GLOW STICK

A Guide to God after Grief

Sabrina Vaz

ARCHWAY
PUBLISHING

Archway Publishing books may be ordered
through booksellers or by contacting:

Archway Publishing
1663 Liberty Drive
Bloomington, IN 47403
www.archwaypublishing.com
844-669-3957

ISBN: 978-1-6657-2615-3 (sc)
ISBN: 978-1-6657-2613-9 (hc)
ISBN: 978-1-6657-2614-6 (e)

Library of Congress Control Number: 2022912294

Print information available on the last page.

Archway Publishing rev. date: 07/21/2022

DEDICATION

To my beautiful daughter,
Tagan Vaz-Barros.
You are my reason.
&
To all the widows who have loved and lost.
May you all find your "glow."

CONTENTS

PREFACE

My story is much like the story of every woman grieving a spouse, yet it is only my story. Each woman who has loved and lost has her own unique narrative. If you are a widow, you have experienced some or all the following emotions: anger, loneliness, fear, confusion, guilt. You may have even felt like there were no more good days ahead for you. Perhaps you still feel that way. I felt all those things and more. It is not an easy road to walk because we feel like there is no longer anyone walking alongside us, holding our hand. But we are not alone. I am not talking about the well-meaning family and friends who always have opinions on how and what we should be doing. I'm talking about God. We can easily become depressed, stop taking care of ourselves, develop health problems. Worst of all, we can give up all hope. But through God, we find the love and the strength to continue down the path of promise.

My second husband, Ricardo, died five years ago. The years of his illness and the time after he passed were challenging for me. I still miss him every day, and although some of the events leading up to his death are a blur, there are many vivid memories and certain ones that still haunt me. But I survived by the grace of God, and I flourished with his love.

I am a widow twice; both of my husbands died of terminal cancer. It doesn't matter if you lost your spouse to cancer, a sudden accident, some other terminal disease, suicide, or violence. Our experience is unique and quite different to one another, yet we have had similar journeys. My desire is to let you know you are not alone; your feelings are valid whatever they may be, and there is a purpose within the pain.

I pray that my testimony will touch you with tears, laughter, and, most important, with aspiration. Yes, a desire to continue to live, to love, and to shine through with God's mercy and light.

1
MEMORIES

M*y memories from that day are blurry. But I can recollect* standing in my new black pumps, with the burgundy suede toes that hurt so bad. My feet were red and swollen when I was finally able to take the shoes off. I also remember the faint scent of lilies dancing around the room. It came from the lovely arrangement of flowers that decorated the perimeter of the coffin that I avoided turning to.

If you asked what the weather was like that day, I wouldn't be able to tell you. I wouldn't really be able to describe the room, the color of the walls, or much of anything else about my surroundings. I am certain that my daughter, Tagan, was standing on my left side. There was a sea of people, some I knew, some unfamiliar, and others I should have recognized but just couldn't.

They told me later the line was out the front door of the funeral home and around the entire building. Police officers had to come to direct cars. He would have liked that. He would have felt that the large turnout was, in some way, a sign of respect. It was warranted. I don't really know too many people who did so much for their community, gave so much, and spread love as much. I guess that's one of the reasons I just couldn't make sense of it.

All I could do was stand there, shoulders pulled down, stomach in, and shake each person's hand when they got to me. I would gently nod as I mouthed "thank you" when they told me how sorry they were. I believed that is what he would have wanted me to do. I wanted to be strong for him.

A few people who glanced over toward the coffin told me how handsome he looked. I didn't want to turn my head. I knew how good looking he was. Even right after his surgery, where they shaved his head on one side and left that horrible scar, he was still such a gorgeous man. Such a beautiful mind lost. I really couldn't understand why God had taken him from me.

The next day wasn't any easier. Standing in the church, I didn't really hear the service. I was forced to stare at the casket knowing he was inside. Understanding that I would never hear his raspy voice tell me he loved me again. I felt so lonely, scared, vulnerable, and broken as the choir sang "Amazing Grace."

When it was finally over, I followed behind the pallbearers as they carried the casket draped in red, white, and blue to the large, gleaming black hearse. I knew it wasn't customary, but I rode in the hearse with him. It was the last car trip we would ever take together. I could hear the driver providing small talk. I just nodded because I was trying to hold on to all that was left—the memories.

> Finally, brethren, whatsoever things are true, whatsoever things are honest, whatsoever things are just, whatsoever things are pure, whatsoever things are lovely, whatsoever things are of good report; if there be any virtue, and if there be any praise, think on these things.
>
> —Philippians 4:8 (KJV)

I remembered someone telling me at my grandfather's funeral that if I kept his memory alive inside of me, he was alive. At sixteen, it was difficult to comprehend, but now as a mature woman widowed twice, it was clear. My memories could keep him alive in my heart. Sometimes we try not to remember the people we loved and lost. There are various reasons we do this, but cherishing the good times are valuable, healing, and do not mean we are trying to live in the past.

Sometimes memories are painful. When we think of our loved ones, we see them as they were before they passed—struggling and sick. It hurts to relive those times, so we block them out. It is also normal when you are grieving, especially when the grief is new, to have an inability to concentrate or focus. For me, it was important to find some beautiful memories to hold on to, and it was helpful in the healing. It was my first step in the process of recovery.

Take a moment to close your eyes and collect your thoughts. Remember a day where you were someplace special with your beloved. It could be a vacation on the beach, a favorite restaurant, or a time spent in your house. Try to bring yourself back to that day. Think about what sights and sounds were around you. How did the air smell? Hear what was said or simply feel the touch of your hand in the hand of your beloved.

Memories are a gift that God gave us. They can never be taken away. We don't want to live in the past, but we don't want to forget it either. The past is part of our history and helps define who we become in the future. Let us make sure that the memories we keep in our hearts forever are ones that bring us peace and pleasure. Use this space to write about that memory, one that makes you smile when you think about your loved one. Visualize that and focus on it.

_____

_____

_____

_____

_____

For me, it was the time we went to Ricardo's favorite steak house right before it permanently closed its doors. The Hilltop Steakhouse was founded in 1961, in Saugus, Massachusetts. Ricardo was three years old when it first opened. It was one of the most popular steak houses in the whole country throughout the 1970s. Until the 1990s, when Americans became more health conscious.

It brought back memories of childhood for both of us. It was a wonderful day, and the lines were heavy. While we waited to be seated, he climbed up on a huge fiberglass cow and flashed his million-dollar smile. He pretended to be Bass Reeves, in his royal blue Aruba sweatshirt, lassoing cattle while he overlooked the congested Route 1 on the north side of Boston. Going back to that memory makes me feel good. I let that picture flash through my mind often—even now.

2

COINCIDENCES

S *haring my story may help you to feel similar emotions of* your own in some way. But this is my account. I was forced to live through the loss twice. As a widow once before, I clearly remembered the feelings of having my life turned upside down. The hurt that is so deep you wonder if you will ever feel anything else again. The thoughts that start to overtake you are, "What do I do *now*? Am I going to survive without him?" And the most pressing question, "Why God?"

But even though I lived through the loss of two loves, each experience was different. You will find differences as well. You will find your own story and your own path. My prayer, as difficult as it seems, is that you may even find a purpose through the pain.

I will tell you, when my first husband passed away, I asked myself those questions every day. Overwhelmed, afraid, and confused, God stepped in and guided me. Shortly after, I met Ricardo. He brought love and joy back into my life. If you are asking yourself similar questions, I will tell you that most widows do survive. If you allow God into your life, he will gently guide you, and as time goes by, he will even reveal the why.

Getting to the point where I could see my husband healthy required a lot of work and reflection. It was really the first step to regaining my physical and emotional health. Once I saw him on that silly cow, I could then picture him standing at the shore casting his fishing pole into the ocean, with all the anticipation of a schoolboy. He would be wearing his Black Dog T-shirt with the frayed collar.

Or he would be sitting at the dark-wood bar inside the Naked Oyster, one of our favorite restaurants. Gleefully chatting with anyone that happened to stroll past him. I was on the path to healing. Those images began to replace the horrific ones of him in bed struggling for breath—weak and in pain.

That journey turned me into a different person. The woman I am today was not the woman I was before Ricardo was diagnosed! That wife and mother that I was came from a young, scared widow left alone to take care of her baby. We are constantly growing and changing. In fact, the person I evolved into is not who I thought I would become. The work can be overwhelming, and sometimes, we make the decision to settle for brokenhearted and broken. You may be reading this and still feeling like you have no more good days ahead of you, or worse, you feel like you do not deserve any more happiness.

You do. I pray every day for everyone, especially women, who experienced a great loss from the death of a spouse, a child, a parent, or even a best friend. My prayer is simple. Listen to God, trust God, and read the testimony of others who had to endure the pain of grief and have healed. So that you, too, may heal. I am hopeful that if you investigate how my loss helped me find my purpose, you may also discover how God wants you to find yours.

Understanding this was challenging for me. It took many reflections on the life I had with my husband. The guilt I felt had to be addressed, so that the anger and the hurt wouldn't be so strong. Those weeks after the funeral were so difficult. My lack of sleep and nourishment caused me to get sick. First it was just a cold, then it got into my chest. Bronchitis, pneumonia, and shingles, it was one thing after another. I was in a very unhealthy place physically and mentally. I had so much to do, but I couldn't do anything except write list after list of things I needed to accomplish. Every morning I got dressed in the same plaid flannel Pendleton shirt that Ric once wore. You may recognize this place.

What I have come to understand is that I was not truly living my purpose before Ric's diagnosis. Pressing the rewind button for a bit, I can recap my days, which were filled with work all except for Sunday, when we would have the big breakfast, put on our best clothes, jump in the car, and drive to church. Monday would roll around again, and I would forget about the word that had been spoken. I rarely had deep conversations with God during the week, and I was "too busy" or "too tired" to pick up my Bible when I would get home from my studio. I was so comfortable in my life with Ricardo that I had forgotten God was supposed to come first.

> God is our refuge and strength,
> A very present help in trouble.
>
> —Psalm 46:1 (KJV)

Coincidently, the same thing had happened before. I would turn to God on my worst days but forget I still needed him on my good days. My life was filled with parallelisms. Before Ric's diagnosis I was finding them everywhere. Weird links to my childhood, first marriage, past chapters that I stored away on the bookshelf in my mind. The first of these occurrences was an innocent friend request.

Growing up a few minutes outside of Boston was wonderful. We were a short train ride to downtown crossing but still lived on the picturesque side of Commonwealth Avenue, once known as the carriage lane. This area allowed us to afford a comfortable home with plenty of room for guests. Although my mother was an only child, my grandmother on my mom's side was Abenaki Indian and French. I called her Nana, and her family was considerably large. One of my cousins on Nana's side was married to a woman named Ruth. She wore her hair straight and free, always falling over her fresh, clean face. One summer she came to visit. Watching her poke around my dad's garden in her flowing ivory linen dress that complemented her tan skin had reminded me of the pictures I looked at in the children's version of the Bible that my grandmother had given me as a gift that year. Eventually, my cousin and Ruth divorced. I grew up and lost contact with both. Ironically, a few months before

Ricardo was diagnosed, I got a Facebook request from a Ruth with a last name I did not recognize. Normally, I do not accept friend requests from someone that I don't know or that doesn't have several of the same contacts. There was something about this woman that I recognized. A lot older, a little weathered, I believe it was my cousin's ex-wife.

Only two books in the Bible are named after women. One of them is the book of Ruth. After connecting on Facebook and exchanging the customary wave, I was for some reason prompted to pull out my Bible. Ruth is a small book that I have read many times. It's so short that I don't think it even takes me fifteen minutes to get through it. As a child I learned kindness matters from Ruth. Now as an adult, rereading it by coincidence, I felt a connection to her because of her life. After ten years, her husband died. She left her country to move with her mother-in-law, Naomi, and she had to make some exceedingly difficult decisions. But in the end, Ruth was rewarded.

I was married to my first husband for a little over ten years. God blessed us with a beautiful daughter, and shortly after she was born, my husband died. It was difficult to come to terms with because cancer is a painful disease not just for the patient but for the caregiver. I thought that my marriage to Ricardo was my reward. Ruth, the woman who married Boaz, not my cousin, stayed in my mind, and the number ten began to bother me for some reason. Ricardo was my friend first before we were engaged, and, just like my first husband, we knew each other for five years before getting married. My engagement to both men was for one year. They say history repeats itself; in my case, it was true.

I am not at all superstitious, yet I do believe there is something to numbers. I thought about forty. Didn't Jesus fast for forty days and forty nights? In Genesis, "rain fell for forty days and forty nights." I could not forget how long Moses was in that desert before God had him lead his people out of slavery.

It was forty years. And what about seven? Isn't that why we as Christians, celebrate the Sabbath. God rested on the seventh day. Because seven is a holy number, the number seven is used a lot in the Bible—fifty-four times in the book of Revelation alone. So, there is something to numbers.

I was married to my second husband twice. The first time in a private ceremony and three weeks later in a beautiful church wedding with an elegant reception following and then the traditional honeymoon. We never really knew which anniversary to celebrate, but somewhere between the two dates—January 22 and February 10—that year, Ricardo and I started planning a trip to Hawaii to commemorate what would soon be our ten-year anniversary. Ten, Ruth. Coincidence or was God whispering something to me?

This trip was going to be a way to recap the magic of our first time on one of the most beautiful places in God's green earth. It was something we both wanted to do. An occasion to look forward to for the next two years. Yes, we had just celebrated our eighth anniversary. Eight, a number in the Bible that represents rebirth. Although my dad died on the eighth year of my life. My grandfather died eight years later. I did not obsess over the number eight. I was too concerned with the number ten.

What does the number ten signify? Well, God did give us the Ten Commandments. Actually, he gave us over 613, but I didn't truly understand that then. Also, when Ricardo and I would pledge our tithe and offerings, we were committing 10 percent of our earnings to the church. The number signifies responsibility and law. It also signifies a completeness, and that's what I was getting worried about.

I didn't want my relationship with my husband to end. I didn't want him to leave me. I didn't want history to repeat itself. I loved my life. It was comfortable, and we were happy. The thing that was missing was a more personal relationship with God, but I didn't realize it although, after reading Ruth,

I started reading the Bible from Genesis again. This time with fresh eyes and in doing so I felt that God wanted to be involved in my life, in Ricardo's life, and the lives of my family and not just when we went to church or said grace before dinner.

Was it a coincidence that my cousin's ex-wife sent me that request? Moreover, was it even her? I don't know if it was, or if God was speaking to me. Was it God's way of getting me to pick up my Bible? The word "coincidence" is used in the Bible only once. It's in the book of Luke, and Jesus uses it when he teaches the parable of the Good Samaritan. What did that have to do with anything? Was I supposed to take solace in knowing that after being left beaten and naked, the traveler was found by the Samaritan, and therefore if I am broken down once again, someone will come to my rescue?

Do you ever go back and question events leading up to the loss that you have endured? It is okay to do that. Regardless of the circumstances surrounding the death of our loved ones, it has a profound influence on us. You may have lost your loved one in an unanticipated incident or, like me, a life-threatening illness. Regardless, the loss is traumatizing. Reviewing the incidents leading up to the death can be beneficial. For me it helped me to understand that there was no fault on my part and that I could use his death in a meaningful way to help others.

Sit comfortably, with your eyes closed, and reflect on the incidents leading up to the loss. Then say this simple prayer:

Father God,

Sometimes I don't feel like I have the strength or the words to pray.

Sometimes I just don't know what to say.

Please help me remember that you want to hear from me and that you want me to heal.

Give me the strength to regain a healthy,
productive, and prosperous life.

Help me to focus on the gratitude I feel to have
had my loved one in my life.

Allow me to keep my loved one's memory alive.

And undertake actions to help bring meaning
to the death.

While I am renewed with purpose.

In your name,
Amen

I said this prayer many times in the three years before I
started writing this book. Yes, it took me that long to find the
peace in my heart, the ability to stay focused and strong enough
to put the story down on paper. Grief has no expiration date.
It is just like love. Recovery is a relative term; we are always
experiencing good days and bad days. I still grieve, but the
intensity has diminished. You may not believe that you can get
to this place, where you know what you need to do and that
you will survive. You will. In fact, you may even understand
God's plan.

3
THE BEGINNING

remember the first time I woke up at three thirty in the morning; it was out of sound sleep. No rain was pounding down from the sky; no lightning flashing above our bed; no sound at all. The cats hadn't disturbed me either. It was just this feeling that washed over me—a feeling of fear that penetrated deep in my gut and rightfully so. The bed was cold and empty. I shifted my feet around on the wood floor trying to find my house slippers. Groggy and tired, I looked in the bathroom where all I found was my fuzzy black robe, which I wrapped around me. For a moment my heart was in my stomach. Scared and confused, I climbed the stairs to his den where an array of video games beckoned to Ricardo many a late night. He was not there either. Finally, I found him sitting on the couch in the dark staring at the gray television screen in our family room. That night was the first of many nights where we congregated in front of the television. Sometimes we watched old movies, and sometimes the TV wasn't even on.

Our middle of the night family room dates became the new normal. This started about a month after "Ruth." He just couldn't sleep. He told me it was his asthma bothering him. The fact that we were getting close to our ten-year anniversary was in the back of my head. I tried many ways to help keep Ric comfortable. I ordered a large wedge pillow to prop him up with, from Amazon. We left soft, soothing music on sometimes IZ who we only discovered on our honeymoon to Hawaii. Lavender aromatherapy was suggested, so I sprayed it around the room, I googled how to sleep with chest pain. Nothing worked. It only got worst.

The doctor kept saying it was heartburn. Talk about numbers; he presented over fifteen times at the doctor's office. Zantac, Nexium, Prilosec were just a few of the medications decorating his nightstand. They were not new to him; Ric had been taking them off and on since I met him. One of our first dates I remember he asked if I wanted a purple pill. My heart sunk because I really liked him.

"I'm sorry, I don't do drugs."

He laughed so hard. "No, it's for heartburn."

I didn't need that because I had never experienced it. But I had observed him struggle with acid reflux and asthma our entire marriage; apparently, he left the Marine Corps with both. I was very health conscious and ate mostly a plant-based menu until we were married. Although I taught exercise, wellness in all facets interested me. When my diet changed by adding meat and other things back, so did my body. Around the same time that he was having trouble sleeping, I decided I should try to lose a few pounds with a juice cleanse. I was working hard at watching what I ate. My husband wasn't, but the number on the scale was going down so much easier for him than it was for me.

This worried me as well, and when he had to go yet again to the doctor, instead of showing concern, the doctor applauded his weight loss. Ironically, we both looked phenomenal. The Figawii ball was right around the corner, and we attended every year. The ball is connected to the Figawii race from Cape Cod to Nantucket. It's also a big fund-raiser for the hospital and the perfect excuse to get dressed up. Seeing my handsome husband in his tux was a treat. Picking out a new dress was also something I enjoyed. That year I wore a floor length black silk gown that was a quite simple design with a plunging back that came to a point right below my scapula's; my hair was pulled up in an elegant twist, and my neck displayed a beautiful diamond that I was usually too nervous to wear. Banquet tables surrounded the perimeter of the ballroom just as they always did and each one offered delicious delicacies from different local restaurants. The food made the event worth the price of admission. He hardly ate. We danced only once that night and got tons of compliments on how great we looked.

"Are we just getting old?"

I wasn't tired; I could have gone another round, so to speak. But I just smiled," Maybe."

I didn't care that we left early; I was content. When the valet pulled our car up, Ric looked over at me and said, "Do you know that this was our tenth Figawii Ball?"

His words caught in my throat. "You don't say, Babe."

I tried to put that out of my head. We were happy together in love, and it had been a lovely night. Why would I question if that could have possibly been our last ball? I have in some way always craved stability, predictability. For me that equaled contentment. I couldn't explain it then, and I still can't. It was almost like God was whispering to me, letting me know I had to be prepared because that security wasn't going to be there too much longer. Some of you may call it intuition. Whatever it was, was causing me to feel nervous, even a bit upset though everything continued as per usual. After the Figawii, we sat in the family room curled up together making plans for the warmer months ahead.

Memorial Day came to kick off the summer on Cape Cod. The beaches were open. The seasonal residents were returning in their Bentley convertibles wearing neatly pressed shorts embroidered with whales, along with the weekly tourists. The hydrangea was suddenly in full bloom, and the sun always seemed to shine bright. We were lunching with friends, booking rides over to the Vineyard and preparing for our annual Fourth of July party. It was Ricardo's favorite holiday, and he did it well with over a hundred family and friends in attendance, decorations, music, fireworks, and a summertime feast.

July 3, we went to a new little breakfast spot with reclaimed wood tables and freshly grown herbs in the raised beds out in front. He ordered the homemade sausage with two eggs over easy. The color of the meat was a strange pinkish gray, and it looked uncooked. We barely were able to pull the car into the garage before Ricardo threw up the entire meal.

That was the first time he vomited after eating. His doctor dismissed the complaint and thought nothing of the fact that throwing up meals became a regular thing too. The uncooked round rare sausage patty haunts me to this day and along with understanding the dietary laws of Leviticus, it made it easy for me to give up pork altogether.

I started having these horrible thoughts, or maybe they were nightmares that one day I would just get this call that he had a heart attack. It was obvious to me something was wrong even though his doctor disagreed. Never in my wildest dreams would I believe it could be cancer. What's that expression? Lightning never strikes twice.

Ricardo had a successful law practice with one office on Old Kings Highway in a stately home that was once a sea captain's manor and was converted into several offices. A lovely building furnished with tasteful antiques from the mid-1700s. it was showcased on some television program listing haunted places across the United States and is a stop on the Haunted Halloween Stroll during October. Not that I believed any of that nonsense. The second office is in the sixth largest city in Massachusetts. Nicknamed "the Whaling City" because it was the world's most important whaling port during the nineteenth century, New Bedford was a busy practice, and it was there about two years earlier that a Cape Verdean man by the name of Antonio Gomes first hired my husband. I cannot disclose the particulars of his lawsuit, but it was one of my husband's biggest cases, and it was going to trial toward the end of the summer. It was scheduled to be heard in the same courtroom in which the infamous Hernandez trial was housed. Ricardo still could not sleep through the night; I taught myself not to either. His other symptoms included weight loss, severe heartburn, and vomiting. Doctor Finn told him it was stress due to the upcoming trial.

Glorious sun-filled days on the beach, drinks on the water, dinner on our back deck with family visiting the Cape, drives to the national seashore and P-town an outdoor concert. Then much before we were ready, summer ended, as well as the trial. After a fifteen-minute deliberation, the jury came back with a not guilty.

It was as if Ricardo sensed something was wrong too. "Babe, if that's my last trial, I did a good job."

"You did more than a good job; you're going to have clients coming out of the woodwork. Why would that be your last trial?"

Nothing changed in September except my age. My birthday was on a Thursday that year, and I had to work. Just like always, Ricardo wanted to spoil me. He discovered this beautiful restaurant on the water off Narraganset Bay, and that weekend we took a romantic drive down along the coast; he drove with one hand in mine and one hand on the wheel. Dinner would have been spectacular but for watching him move his food from side to side on the plate unable to eat anything, seeing him play with the straw in his cocktail but not drink any was upsetting. We were supposed to continue down to Newport. I could see how tired he was, thin and drawn but still handsome. I drove back that night. When we got home, I read the book of Ruth again looking for comfort.

Is there a person in the Bible who resonates with you? Is there a scripture that has always had a way of offering you comfort? What about a Bible story that you feel a connection to? Take the time to mediate on it or perhaps read a few verses in your Bible and see what happens. The Bible has a way of offering us reassurance when we are going through tough times. After all, it is a guidebook in some way. Once you find a verse or a scripture, copy it in the space below or write about how it connected with what you are feeling. After completing this, you may want to continue copying scripture that brings you solace.

_____

_____

_____

_____

_____

_____

The courage, the faith, and the goodness of God in the book of Ruth really resonated with me during that time. It still does. I realize now her story inspired me to build my own spiritual legacy. And like Ruth, the book doesn't end with a wedding; it ends with a grandmother rocking her beautiful grandson. There is a lot more to my story, and it continues past this book. I am not jumping the gun, as they say, but so does yours.

> And Ruth said, Intreat me not to leave thee, or to return from following after thee: for whither thou goest, I will go; and where thou lodgest, I will lodge: thy people shall be my people, and thy God my God.
> —Ruth 1:16–17 (KJV)

4
THE NIGHTMARE

> For all flesh is as grass, and all its glory of man as the flower of grass. The grass withereth, and the flower therof falleth away.
>
> —1 Peter 1:24 (KJV)

L ife is such a strange and fragile thing. We witness this in our daily life without paying any mind to it. Every Thursday, I would stop by this roadside farm stand with a small selection of fresh garden-variety tomatoes, which I would overlook, place my eight crumpled dollar bills in the rusty old cash box and carefully select two stems of tall stargazer lilies. They would sit on the side table in the living room where our cats never ventured. By Saturday, several flowers would be in full bloom, exposing magnificent free-form brush strokes. Sunday would reveal the birth of the last few bulbs. By Wednesday the scent no longer lingered through the house, and petals bright white only a few days earlier were now a drab brown as they floated onto the table waiting for me to dispose of them. We buy fresh fruit and vegetables that we don't always consume, watch them rot in our refrigerator, then throw them away without thinking anything of it. The delicate cycle of life and death surrounds us daily. Every breath we take seems like such a small thing. We don't know when our last exhale will happen. It was becoming exceptionally clear to me that Ricardo was struggling to complete the simple act of breathing that often is taken for granted. After the haunting comment he made about the Gomes trial, I was certain he knew it as well. But the doctor's office showed no concern for any of his complaints.

They say we write to relive our experiences. They say we write to remember. I didn't need to write this for either one of those reasons. My late husband, Ricardo "Ric" Barros, will always live in my heart, and those days leading up to his diagnosis couldn't possibly be forgotten.

Just like the image I will always have of him sitting in his tattered royal blue "Gone fishing" T-shirt and his favorite denim jeans that were now too big, slumped over on the peaty soil in our garden trying so hard to dig the last few potatoes of the season. It was the morning after my birthday dinner, preoccupied with my dahlias. I had cut enough that our large red Kenyan basket purchased up in Wellfleet was overflowing with purple, hot pink, crimson, yellow, and white blooms. I didn't notice him until I walked around past the grates covered in vines of various varieties of tomatoes like the little Sun Gold cherry tomatoes, we both liked to pluck and eat.

"Babe, what happened?"

"I want to make some kale soup, and I need these potatoes." He paused. "I just got so out of breath." I could hear him struggling as though he was having an asthma attack.

Maybe I was wrong, and he had developed a very severe case of COPD. I prayed to God as I pulled him off the ground. I prayed as I brought the basket to the car and opened the heavy metal gate to drive our old SAAB up to our plot where I left him resting on a bench that someone had put together with two tree stumps. I prayed every morning and every night.

That evening I made his grandmother's kale soup with the potatoes and vegetables that we had grown. Ric sat at the counter teaching me how to roll and cut the leafy green kale long and thin in the pot just as he had watched her do. When it was ready, we poured the flavorful soup into our best bowls, enjoying every spoonful. He kept it down as well.

One of the places I feel most connected to my late husband is the kitchen. There are days still now where I live in Richmond when I chop an onion or mince a clove of garlic, I can feel him over my shoulder. Certain cookbooks, the ones with the little sauce stains on them, I love the most because I know those are recipes he made. I have always loved to cook but I was never as good at it as my husband was. I feel like after he passed, I got better at it because I had him telling me how to hold the knife or what to add or subtract. Think about places or activities that help you feel connected to your loved one. These are ways to continue a bond with a spouse.

Many therapists, grief support groups, and self-help books tell us we must focus on moving on, accepting the loss, closure. I disagree. Keeping a bond with our loved one is not unhealthy, and it doesn't mean that we cannot move on. Many times, throughout my second marriage, I experienced connections with my first husband. There was and is still a comfort in that.

Here are a few ways I was able to do this: (1) Sometimes big decisions can be difficult. I often imagine what advice Ricardo would offer me. I have even had dialogue with him. When I was faced with the decision of soaking more money into his SAAB or selling it, talking the decision through, and imagining what he would have told me helped me come to terms with letting it go. (2) We are always meeting new and important people. Eventually perhaps new relationships will enter our life as well. It's okay to introduce these new people to your loved one that passed away with a special story you feel comfortable sharing about your spouse. After moving to Richmond, I made some new friends; through my stories they understand who my husband was. (3) There may have been an activity you were planning to do together; it's okay to complete that in your loved one's memory. We spoke about redoing our master bath many times. Finances were difficult after the loss, but I was able to complete a remodeling with a little barter from my studio. (4) Special photos of the person you loved and lost are okay to have around. You don't want to turn your entire home into a shrine, but a picture that makes you smile should be on display. I have a special photo of the two of us in my living room. It was taken the night we attended our first Figawii Ball. (5) Did you both have a special trip planned? It's okay to make plans to take that trip without your spouse. Although I have not done it, I am saving for a trip to Hawaii with our daughter. (6) Memorialize his (or her) Facebook page. Facebook has a process to support you in doing this. It was easy, and now family and friends can visit his page and post. (7) Finish a project that they were working on before they passed. Perhaps it was simply cleaning up the garage or rearranging the family room. For me, cleaning up became necessary because I moved, but I knew he would have loved that I reorganized stuff. (8) Take up a hobby that your late husband enjoyed. Ricardo introduced me to so many new experiences, gardening, fishing, boating, clamming. The first two I continue to do on my own. I feel really connected to him when I am in the soil or by the water. (9) Keep a few special items that belonged to your spouse around you. In Ricardo's law office, he had a brass bear standing tall on a round mahogany platform; the sculpture rested on his bookcase. Lovingly he would tell me he was my big brown bear. When I had to clean out his law office, it was one of the special items I kept. (10) Celebrate your anniversary by purchasing a gift for yourself. Years ago, I had a client that had lost her husband. Every year on what would have been their wedding anniversary, she would treat herself to something special. One year it was a new rug, another anniversary she proudly displayed a painting she purchased of her favorite beach. It brought her joy thinking of something that would have a deep meaning for both as her anniversary approached. This past year I took a lesson from her and purchased a new laptop that I really needed. My old laptop was given to me by Ricardo.

In Ecclesiastes 9:5 (KJV) we are told "the dead know not a thing, neither have they any more a reward; for the memory of them is forgotten." However, I believe what King Solomon was saying was that the physical body is forgotten. The spirit of our loved one is different. We can gain strength and knowledge from their spirit. Just as we learn in Deuteronomy 32:7 (KJV), "Remember the days of old, consider the years of many generations: ask thy father, and he will shew thy elders, and they will tell thee." In other words, it's not wrong for us to turn to the spirit of our loved ones that are no longer with us.

Most importantly remember, do what feels right to you. Family members, friends, therapists—they are all quick to tell us how to grieve. There is not one way or a right way. We cannot understand the grieving process because it is different for each of us; therefore, we must do what helps us to move through one of the most difficult times of our life. If you really want advice, then ask God in your daily conversation and prayer with him.

On Friday that week, Ricardo left for work early. It was October 2. I will always remember that day. He returned to the house around 11:30 a.m. with a bottle of Ensure. I was just returning from my studio as well. Dressed in his tan suit with the light-yellow shirt and the yellow vineyard vines tie I had picked up for him, he looked good.

"I met this man today—it was a horrible story." He placed the can on the cold brown granite over our center island and sat on one of the stools.

"It broke my heart to tell him I couldn't help him. Both he and his sister lived on the base I was stationed at for six months. You remember, Camp Lejeune in North Carolina?"

I nodded. He continued, "Well, his sister has leukemia, and he was diagnosed with liver cancer."

"How horrible." I could feel the color leaving my face.

"Their father was stationed there, and the cancer is related to the contaminated water that they drank when they were kids."

It was as if an arrow pierced me right between the eyes. The palm of my hand pressed to my forehead. No words were forming, as my mind was trying to process the word *contaminated*. Camp Lejeune was where Ricardo was stationed as a young marine. He was at the base for three years. Three years of drinking contaminated water, bathing in contaminated water. This guy had only been there with his sister and his dad for six months; now they both had some sort of cancer.

"Where is the dad now?" I don't even know why I asked.

"He passed away a few years back."

"Babe, you were there for three years."

His eyes were gray and drawn. "I know. I got a letter that President Obama had sent out about a year ago, and I brought it over to Doctor Finn."

He opened the can of Ensure. "He checked me out and said I was fine."

I felt a little more relaxed. "Okay, good. What tests did he run?"

I grabbed a big, plastic, amber-colored glass from the cupboard and poured the chalky liquid in. I added a few ice cubes and slid it across the counter.

"I don't remember that he ran any tests, but he said I was fine. It's just this asthma thing; that's why I'm going to try this drink." He ran his long finger over the top of the glass.

"It really did break my heart to say I couldn't help that guy and his sister today. You know the water was contaminated for thirty-four years. We didn't just drink it; we bathed in it too. The USMC leaders knew about it, and they never said a damn word. But I'm still glad I served my country. It was Obama that finally did something about it." He lifted the drink up to his lips and guzzled down every drop.

"Down the hatch, Babe. The quicker you drink something—" he pushed the stool out from under him and ran into the bathroom without finishing his sentence.

I remember screaming, "Oh my God" and running after him. Within seconds there was throw up everywhere and swimming in the vomit were pieces of undigested kale. The kale from a week ago. His food wasn't being processed. I also knew he wasn't going to the bathroom regularly anymore. I could feel tears in my eyes, and I tried to push them back.

Tagan came downstairs and saw the toilet and floor covered, "Daddy, what happened?"

That evening at work, a text message flashed across my iPhone while I was teaching a large group class. Ricardo was letting me know he was directly admitted to the hospital on Cape Cod. He said to come right over as soon as I could. My heart was beating so fast as I closed the door of my studio. My hand was shaking as I turned the key in the lock. Somehow, I kept it together when Tagan asked me where we were going:

"Honey, Daddy is in the hospital."

I saw the tears, shiny and wet, on her pale, clear skin. "Is he going to be, okay?"

"We just have to pray."

Hospitals are always so cold and sterile. We walked past walls decorated with beautiful scenic oceans painted with colors of orchid and teal, but they didn't help. My heels clicked; Tagan's sneakers squeaked against the industrial linoleum. It was the only sound. We found Ricardo's room empty, but by the time we took off our jackets, a gurney was being wheeled into the room.

I wanted to scream. I wanted cry. A thin bald man in hospital scrubs helped him up and into the bed. My big, strong, handsome husband looked frail. He had aged just from the morning. Nine pounds of fluid was drained from his stomach. That was more than my daughter weighed when she was born. She had only been six pounds seven ounces.

I was sitting on one side of the bed, and Tagan was on the other. We were all holding hands when a cute, spunky nurse in a baggy top covered in pumpkins came in announcing she was the administering nurse, and she had some questions. Ricardo wanted to know where she was from, joked with her, and basically was his usual charming self. Her name was Jess

Hinckley. Turned out that he had represented her older sister in a divorce case a few years back. Watching the way, he interacted with her calmed me down. His spirits were high; maybe he was feeling better. Maybe this was a good thing because they got it—whatever it was.

Jess passed a doctor on her way out of the room.

"Mr. Barros, is this your wife?"

"Yes, my wife, Sabrina, and my daughter, Tagan."

It was a blockage. There was a procedure called the Bill Roth II. The doctor would arrange for my husband to be brought up to Brigham & Women's Hospital in Boston for the surgery. It was a good hospital with some of the finest doctors in the country. The absolute best news was that there was no cancer.

5
THE C WORD

> Wherein ye greatly rejoice, though now for a season, if need be, ye are in heaviness through manifold temptations: That the trial of your faith, being much more precious than of gold that perisheth, though it be tried with fire, might be found unto praise and honour and glory at the appearing of Jesus Christ.
>
> —1 Peter 1 6–7 (KJV)

t is hard to understand how our trials and tribulations somehow benefit us while we are living through them. I look back now and realize that I was being tested. We are taught so many life lessons. Do we remember them? Reading scripture is one thing, but do we apply what we learn? Do we express our gratitude to God each day regardless of the favor he shows upon us? Sometimes we cannot see the blessing in the way the Lord intended us to. We may even feel as though we are being cursed.

The love my husband and I shared was true. We chose each other in the beginning and continued to choose each other every day through the beauty and sanctity of marriage. Our amazing daughter was a blessing, the house we lived in, the cars we drove, everything was blissfully ordinary. I appreciated my life. I was grateful, yet I took it all for granted, never thinking that what I had was everything I wanted. Was that selfish? Was it a sin? I desperately wanted to make sense of it all, and I tried to find a way to take the blame. I wondered if I was being punished. Recognizing the why of it is difficult, I'm sure you questioned the circumstances as your life was changing around you in a comparable way. These are common thoughts even for Christians. We need to remember death is a natural process of life as well. Before reading any further, please take a moment to say another short prayer of simple gratitude. There is power in prayer.

Father God,

Without you I have nothing.

Every perfect gift has come from you.

These are things I have come to believe I deserve.

Help me to have a grateful heart, to continue to thank you for the time I had with my loved one.

And all the blessings you have bestowed upon me.

I ask you to help me recognize these as such.

And to recognize that life is constantly changing.
I too am evolving.

This can be a gift if I allow it to be so.

In Jesus's name,
Amen.

Ricardo was admitted to Brigham & Women's Hospital on Francis Street in Boston on the following Wednesday. I wanted to believe what the doctor told me on Cape Cod—an ulcer. He looked too sick, too weak and I was angry at myself for thinking that. Tired and lonely, I missed him around the house—the delicious meals he would have prepared when I got home from work and curling up on the long burgundy couch together. I hated sleeping alone and not being able to share conversation over a morning cup of coffee; I missed all those things that had just seemed customary. Now nothing was as it should be. Eating—the necessary act of cooking a light meal and sitting down to consume it—became so difficult. Family members came and went in and out of the house. They didn't comfort me; instead, they just helped me to realize how much my world had changed. I wanted to be with my husband. I drove the ninety minutes up Route 93 fighting the daily congestion that Bostonians are used to dealing with every day even though he told me I didn't have to. Everyone else told me I would wear myself out. Regardless, I had to visit for my own sanity. Just to feel his hand around mine, to look into his deep brown eyes not knowing if that could be the last time.

His surgery was set for the following Tuesday because it was Columbus Day weekend. A lot of doctors had off, including the one scheduled for Ricardo's procedure. We would have gone away as well. We went to the White Mountains every fall to leaf peep, to hike up this little path that led to the silence of an icy waterfall where we would sit on large granite boulders watching God's instillation. Later we would meander through white tents filled with local craftmanship and then eat some culinary masterpiece at "Gypsy Café." It was always a glorious weekend, and I felt blessed. I just didn't realize how special those long New Hampshire weekends really were until they became impossible.

Dr. Clancy was a young man with kind eyes hidden behind gold rimmed bifocals. He seemed caring, attentive, and, most importantly, he knew what he was doing. Not only did he perform the gastrojejunostomy regularly; he taught the procedure to young interns from Harvard. Basically, Ricardo had the best in the business. I was relieved and worried at the same time. It's nicknamed the Billroth II, and it is usually used for patients with severe ulcers just like the one they said Ric had. I wanted to believe there was nothing to worry about, told myself I was being silly, but my gut instinct told me differently.

The Saturday morning before the surgery, I woke up at 4:00 a.m. and couldn't go back to sleep. One of my brothers-in-law was staying with me and my sister-in-law, Brenda, who

I am very close with to this day. They were all asleep, including Tagan. I got out of bed very early, showered, pulled on my black cable knit sweater dress and my rubber Burberry boots. My hair was still wet; I stuck it up in a hat and off I went to our garden. It was Ricardo's happy place, which was why I loved it there so much too. I guess gardens make you think of birth, growth, life. I needed that type of therapy. The sun was peeking out from behind the trees on the western side, and the air smelled clean and fragrant as I dug around in the dirt. Even though it was mid-October my dahlias were still in full bloom. I picked a few tomatoes and cut enough flowers to make a lovely arrangement for Ricardo. It was so tranquil there in those two little plots that we got to till and plant in that community garden. I paused with my basket hooked over my right arm and shears and gloves in my left hand. I had never really looked at it. I never really took it all in—how lucky I was too be in that place. Not the garden, not just to have the opportunity to grow our own food, to be married to a man I love, to have a beautiful daughter, to smell the clean Cape air in autumn. I desperately didn't want the winds of change to swoop down on my life and blow it all to bits.

I had a plan. It was to grow old with Ricardo, make enough money to spend part of the winters in Aruba and spoil our grandkids. I was extremely attached to that, but it didn't align with God's plan. I had faith and yet I felt threatened, felt like my life was changing, and I wasn't ready for that change.

So many people came to visit that weekend, which also worried me. His sister and her family from Chicago drove all the way to Boston, another brother flew in from Arizona. Did they suspect something as well? He was exhausted although he maintained good spirits. The surgery was scheduled for 6:00 a.m. on Tuesday. His sister Brenda rented a hotel room right down the street for Monday night. We had a nice visit with Ricardo. Then we went to dinner at this great Tapas restaurant on Newbury Street. The weather was mild for October, and we sat at a sidewalk bistro table in light sweaters, ordered various little plates with olives, cheese, potatoes and a bottle of red wine. When it came, I recognized the label immediately, it was the same merlot we served at our wedding. Convinced this was a sign and everything would be fine, I drank more than I was used to drinking although it may have been for the best because back in the room, I could hear Brenda talking as I drifted off into a much-needed deep sleep better than I had in months.

We could wake up and go right over to the hospital; yet somehow, we were still the last ones to get to his room. My husband was one of sixteen kids. One of his older brothers had already passed away the year before we got married. Four of his other brothers were there with us. Thankfully, I got to talk to him before he was wheeled down to surgery. I got to kiss him, tell him how much I love him, and hear him say he loved me.

Right before they took him, he slid off his wedding ring and put it on my finger. "I can't keep this during surgery, but I want it back as soon as I get out." He winked at me.

We were told the operation would take almost eight hours. There was a comfortable family room in Brigham & Women with reclining couches in soothing tan leather; TVs hung randomly around the sterile room that was also adequately appointed with magazines, games, and even baskets filled with yarn and knitting needles—all the things that could aid in occupying the nervous families that eagerly awaited the news of the outcome of their loved ones. Although I enjoyed reading, I couldn't focus on anything, including the Bible, since Ricardo was first admitted into the hospital. I had brought a red waterproof tote bag a friend had given me for my birthday from the Met filled with several books on various subjects that I once thought interesting, my journal, which I wrote in every day, and the needlepoint that I was working on. I never touched any of it. Instead, I nervously played with my rings, spinning them around my finger and flicking my acrylic nails against one another making an annoying sound that probably irritated everyone around me. The small hand on my watch hit 11:00 a.m., which offered a false sense of relief and made me realize I hadn't gone to the bathroom in close to six hours. I knew Dr. Clancy was more than halfway through with the surgery. It was safe to make my way to the bathroom down the hall.

I had just gone in when my daughter came pounding at the door to inform me the surgeon was looking for me. I pulled up my pants and, in the rush, dumped the contents of my gray suede bag all over the cold linoleum floor. My heart was racing, and my head told me it wasn't good. I prayed as I scurried following her back to the waiting area.

Doctor Clancy was waiting for me, seated on the edge of one of the couches. The television set that dangled from a thin black bracket behind him was muted. I reluctantly sat across from him in a large tan armchair. I felt my eyes meet his in what was a pleading attempt to not have his lips express my biggest fear.

He looked uneasy, and he called me Mrs. Barros. "Your husband is resting comfortably."

Nervously he played with the corner of the long white jacket he was wearing with his name neatly embroidered on the left breast pocket. "I had to close him back up."

He swallowed. "The cancer is everywhere. It's pretty aggressive, and it's already encroaching on his pancreas."

There it was—the C word. I heard it clearly. That wasn't the worst of it. The doctor also mouthed the word *pancreas*. Years ago, when my first husband was sick with lung cancer, I went in to get my hair trimmed. The hairdresser, a woman only about ten years older than I was, who I had known for a long time, told me she was diagnosed with pancreatic cancer. That was my last haircut with her; six weeks later, she had passed away.

I was briskly cupping my right fist into my left hand as

my upper body rocked back and forth, tears sliding down my cheeks in an unending stream. I could hardly breath. The pain in my chest was an intense stabbing that I had never known before.

"Doctor Clancy, are you saying its pancreatic cancer?"

"No, Mrs. Barros, it's stomach cancer; however, the tumor is so large that it is touching on the pancreas."

I nodded and then I asked, "What stage is it?"

I already figured out that it had to be fairly advanced, but I wanted to know, I needed to know, how bad it was. When he replied that it was stage IV, it was like God had ripped out my heart.

I screamed, "Why God? Why have you done this to me again?"

I knew all my brothers-in-law were in the room. I heard tears and sighs, but I didn't know who had come behind me and tried to comfort me with a hand on my shoulder. I felt numb, paralyzed. Every one of my worst nightmares had come true. My life—my beautiful, normal, comfortable life that I had taken for granted for so long—had been obliterated in one brief conversation with a man I hardly knew. How was that possible?

At that moment, I blamed God. I was filled with fear and weariness. I couldn't imagine how bad my life would get or how I could get the courage and strength to get through it. I didn't understand at that point in my life that I would be victorious through this trying time because Jesus was. I also questioned God's love for me. I felt abandoned and alone even though family surrounded me.

> But thanks be to God, which giveth us the victory through our Lord Jesus Christ.
>
> —1 Corinthians 15:57 (KJV)

6
ACCEPTANCE

B *righam and Women's Hospital is one of the largest research* hospitals in the world. It was the first hospital to complete an organ transplant and successful heart valve procedure. Somehow connected to Harvard University, I knew it was once Peter Bent Brigham Hospital, where my dad had been when I was a child. The reputation of the facility was top rate, and for thirty days, Ric would be recovering from a surgery that didn't help, leaving him weak, with two separate tubes attached to his abdomen and another coming from his nose that somehow went down through his throat, at BWH. He couldn't eat or walk. I visited every day shocked and broken. Sometimes I would wake up early and drive to Boston before the rush of morning and leave around 1:00 p.m. to get back to work. Other times I would work till nine in the evening, then drive up and sleep over in the hospital on the plastic mattress they had brought into the room for me. I was mentally, physically, emotionally exhausted. Everything seemed so unfair.

Most of the time I would sit watching Ric sleep playing with my phone. I started googling stage IV stomach cancer. Survival rates came up. Five percent of people with this horrible disease make it past the five-year mark. Ricardo could be in that small population of people. He would see our daughter graduate from high school. Was that the best we could ask for, five years? My head was flooded with thoughts. The internet wasn't helping; yes, a miracle could happen, I read about them, then there were those situations where the patient didn't even live for six months, I read about that too. I couldn't understand how that doctor on Cape Cod, Doctor Finn, could have misdiagnosed him for so long.

Each day's visit started including a stop in the little chapel on the first floor near the first tower. It was always open—even in the middle of the night. Regardless of the time, I rarely met anyone else visiting the sanctuary. I wasn't talking to God. I was questioning him.

"God, if you love me, why did you do this to me again?"

I was bargaining with God. "If you let my husband, come home, I will promise to spend more time volunteering in church." "Please let us have one more summer together, God. I promise to be a better Christian."

I was in extreme despair, angry and scared, struggling with my faith. Many Christians suffer the temptation of doubt when things seem bleak. After all, Jesus shook questions on the cross—didn't he? I was alone in a place of deep anxiety, so much so that I could hardly eat. My hopes were so fragile—delicate like a beautiful crystal. Any type of impact could force me to crumble and crack.

A few weeks into his stay, my own health was deteriorating. I woke up in the hospital room with a painful migraine. Ricardo thought perhaps I needed coffee, which made sense. I was somewhat dependent on the dark, rich brew. I threw on some clothes and headed up to the cafeteria for my morning cup of Joe. There was a smell when I entered. I'm not sure if it was bacon or just the grease. Whatever it was triggered something deep inside me, and just like a volcano on the big island, vomit erupted and poured all over the linoleum. I was shocked and embarrassed that I did that. Why didn't I try to make it to the bathroom down the hall or at least to the oversized round rubber trash barrel. It was early and not very busy, especially on the weekends. I cleaned the floor myself, laying large bunches of brown paper towels down over the mess, and ran into the bathroom to clean up.

Foolishly, I decided I should eat something to settle my stomach. Eggs scrambled and a small fruit cup seemed innocent enough. My head pounded with each step I took toward the cashier. I paid and made my way to a table in the back by a large window looking out at the stillness of Boston on the weekends. My plastic fork carried a small portion of fluffy yellow to my lips. They tasted bland; I added a bit of black pepper and the entire contents of one package of salt. One more bite, nothing more. Just like that, I felt it happening again. I ran to the rubbish just in time.

Weak and still queasy, I abandoned the rest of the plate, which sat on a brown plastic tray along with the coffee I never drank. The elevator took me back up to Ricardo's room where he was waiting for me.

"What took you so long, Babe."

I started to regale the morning disaster when the feeling came over me again. I darted into his bathroom and covered the entire tiled floor with vomit. The nurse on duty caught me in the act, and before I understood what was going on, I was in a wheelchair being transported to the emergency room on the first floor.

If God calls you to task, he will be there every step of the way. I was overwhelmed; my husband was too. But God was not. Lying on the stretcher behind a flimsy curtain, I was told that they needed to run some tests on me to make sure I didn't have a brain tumor. I could hardly open my eyes, yet I could clearly see pictures flashing before me.

I stood looking off into the distance with a large, brimmed hat cocked just slightly over to one side, a beautiful bouquet of roses and bright purple astilbe in my hands. It was my first wedding. Then I was standing on the rocks watching the waves crash at my feet with my first husband, Nuno, by my side. The hot Portuguese sun was hitting our faces. I remembered that day. Then probably my most cherished picture—my beautiful daughter right after she was born. Fast forward, the picture of Ric and I at the Marine Corps Ball, perhaps too soon after Nuno passed away. Ricardo on one knee on the boardwalk in Miami; our wedding; Hawaii; vacations; happy faces; the three of us sitting by the seven-foot-tall Christmas tree in the family room surrounded by presents; skiing in the mountains; laughing, loving, and comfortable.

"God, what are you trying to tell me?"

I felt a sharp poke and saw a woman in blue scrubs inserting an IV into my left hand. More pictures flashing—us at the Topsfield Fair, us eating ice cream at Four Seas. Another poke. I felt drowsy.

I heard a soft, faint voice—the voice of a man. I couldn't open my eyes. I tried, but I just couldn't; my lids were too heavy. His words were soft, clear, as he promised to restore my soul if I came to him. He told me he knew I was weary; he would give me rest so that I could carry the heavy burden put on me.

I woke to the sensation of a tingling on the bottom of my right foot. Tagan stood at the end of my mattress, saying, "Mama, they said we can go home when you are ready."

Confused and still tired, I asked what time it was. I had slept for over twelve hours on that lumpy emergency room mattress. But for God, I didn't have anything wrong with me other than the fact that I had presented dehydrated, exhausted, and with symptoms of the flu. My brother-in-law drove us home, and I wasn't allowed to visit my husband until the following weekend. We talked every day, and when I told him about the pictures, the voice, the promise, I could hear him smile through my iPhone.

"Get your Bible out and check out Matthew 11:28."

> Come unto me, all ye that labour and are heavy laden, and I will give you rest.
>   —Matthew 11:28 (KJV)

There it was written in black and white, on the pages of my Bible. God had indeed sent an angel to me. I wasn't sure if he was telling me everything would be all right, that he would take care of me? That he would make my husband whole again? Or was he simply telling me he would give me the strength to get through this exceedingly difficult time? Ricardo could see what I was going through. As worried about him as I was, I knew he was worried about me and just as scared. He didn't want to leave the life we had either. He wasn't ready to die. And there he was comforting me as I rested on our long comfortable couch surrounded by our cats, piles of book, and mementos of the love our family shared, allowing my body to prepare for the battle ahead.

"Babe, you must trust God. I can beat this."

Between my experience in the hospital and Ricardo's faith, I was inspired to pray without as much anger and resentment; his trust in God encouraged me to trust God more.

Truthfully, there was so much of which I couldn't make sense. Ric was getting a little stronger but only walking with assistance, sitting up for short periods, and not eating. They told us that they would try chemotherapy and that he would be going home with both the G and J tubes coming out of his abdomen. One was connected to his stomach and was how he got food, and the other to his small bowel. This was how he was being relieved of fluid and bile. I would need to learn how to feed him through one and drain the bag connected to the other tube. I would have to learn to administer meds and stab his thigh with a needle every other day. It was frightening to see him like that.

"Yes, Babe, I trust God. I love you, and I know things will be okay."

> But they that wait upon the LORD shall renew their strength, they shall mount up with wings as eagles; they shall run, and not be weary; and they shall walk and not faint.
>
> —Isaiah 40:31 (KJV)

Praying every day in an entirely different way, thinking about all those pictures that had played in my mind in the hospital too helped me to realize how fortunate, how blessed, I was in my life. So many beautiful times I have experienced. I started to understand that God loves me. God had something planned for me. I added "Dear God, thank you for everything" as I started my dialogue with God every morning.

A few days before Ricardo was scheduled to come home, I went to the garden with my scissors and basket. The ground was hard. Every one of the dahlias had turned black. Just like that, they were gone. I was staring at a life like that. A life that one day could just be gone. Everything that I thought would be, I knew could be ripped away in a minute, and it made my soul tremble. I knew how fragile life is. Those beautiful, bright-colored flowers, vibrant and viable when the sun was setting on them but gone the next morning. Nothing lasts forever; nothing stays the same. Those lovely dahlias were gone only until next spring when I could plant new bulbs. I would then be able to witness life again. The man that I was sharing my bed with was eighty pounds lighter, could not eat or drink, and had taken the Lord as his Savior and had repented of all his sins. He was not the same as he was before being admitted into the hospital. He was still alive. There is a relationship between belief and grief. I was trying hard to understand the complexity of this liaison. If my husband had to be taken from me, he would be with God. Why, then, does the thought of his passing still cause me to ache? If I genuinely believe, then why would I grieve so deeply? Did the depth of my pain mean I wasn't putting all my love and trust in God? This was a process of discovery.

I didn't see it at the time, but the months of Ricardo's illness helped me to find out a lot about myself. For one, I learned I was stronger than I thought. I also discovered my own passions—things that helped me to realize who I was. And of course, most importantly, I learned how to lean on God. Make a list of a few

things that you have discovered about yourself in the time you
have been grieving. Reflect deeply; there are things:

1._____

2._____

3._____

4._____

5._____

> But I would not have you to be ignorant, Brethren,
> concerning them which are asleep, that ye sorrow not,
> even as others which have no hope. For if we believe
> that Jesus died and rose again, even so them also
> which sleep in Jesus will God bring with him.
>
> —1 Thessalonians 4:13 (KJV)

7

REVELATION

There was turmoil in my heart—a wrestling between my desire to trust my faith and the ache deep down in my belly. I no longer questioned God's love for me. I knew that he took care of me that day in the hospital; he gave me the rest I needed to build the strength to prepare myself for the days ahead. From rereading the Bible with fresh eyes, I realized he related to what we feel when our lives are falling apart, when we stand to lose someone, we love so deeply. I had asked myself that question of relating a hundred times when my first husband was suffering. Only after my own experience in the emergency room did I come up with a resounding *yes*! As painful as it was, God allowed Jesus to die for us. Of course, I have always known this fact because I have been a Christian my entire life. Although I have some Evangelical friends who would probably disagree with that statement. I was baptized, went to Sunday school, attended Catholic middle school and High School, I was from a mixed marriage. My mother was a Catholic who, while I was growing up and now again, attends Mass regularly. My father was a Protestant, I believe at an early age Lutheran, and then after his mother died Baptist, because it was the denomination of his stepmother. Knowing the Bible well, he became agnostic as an adult but without question a follower of Christ.

As a child I went through a bit of an identity crisis. I would watch my dad sick in bed with his oversized leatherbound Bible with the frayed binding on top of the other books he was involved in. My mother, however, told me that when she was a child, reading the Bible was forbidden. After my dad passed, along with a small catalog of rocks, his dictionary, and a few art books, I kept his Bible. When my mom would fall asleep rebelliously, I would watch movies or secretly read that large, heavy, leatherbound Bible that once rested on my dad's bed.

When I was seven, my religious teacher had us all go around the room and put "Saint" in front of our names. My best friend at the time sat across from me; she was Saint Elizabeth. Saint

John, Saint Paul, and Saint Joan sat between us. When it was my turn, I paused. There was no Saint Sabrina.

My mom had assured me it was all right because my middle name was Jean, and she was a saint—thank God. The next week in Sunday school, I immediately told Mrs. Door, my teacher, that I was emphatically named after Saint Jean. She wasn't really interested or impressed. Right after Halloween that year, the Christmas pageant cast list was posted. Saint Elizabeth, Saint Joan, and Saint Mary were all picked to be angels. They got to wear the long white robes and the shiny gold wings. I was cast in a lead role, as Judas. That was just the beginning of what would be many disappointments. The following October, on a breezy autumn day after coming home from school with a handmade "get well" card I assembled in art class, I learned my dad had died.

I was then labeled the kid with no dad. The only child whose dad died in my entire school. Somehow it got even worse; I was labeled with many nicknames—none that I wanted to be called. My childhood was tough, but that's another story. I just wanted a place to fit in, to belong. When I became a teenager, I tried to find that special place. I guess you could say I churched hopped. Trying to embrace my Swedish heritage, I attended a Lutheran Church for a period thinking of my dad's family. Later, my first boyfriend was Pentecostal; I would sneak off to church with him without my mom knowing. There was the Baptist Church I visited for a time, the Methodist Church in which I married my first husband, the return to my Catholic roots, and then the nondenominational Protestant Church that Ricardo and I attended.

I mention all this for a few reasons. First, regardless of what church you attend or even if you do not attend church at all and just consider yourself a follower of Christ, we all must read our Bibles. The Bible is our truth. Second, loss is not new to me. There are tragedies all around us. Sometimes when we hear about natural disasters, terrorist attacks, friends who have lost loved ones to terminal disease, or even murder, we are able to offer prayer, compassion, or sometimes just shut our eyes to it. When death is your own reality, its different. I have had the reality of death through my entire life. Here it was again.

The first morning didn't seem like a new day; I had given Ric his meds at 11:00 p.m.; the news played in the background. I drained his bag the way they showed me in the hospital and filled his pump with three cans of a milky substance that smelled a bit like a candy I enjoyed, as a child, Necco wafers. Eight large boxes had been left by the garage while we were still fighting through the rush hour traffic on the commute back home from the hospital. I had forgotten they were there, so after getting Ric into the house and comfortable, unpacking his things, and getting Tagan and the animals fed, I realized I would need to carry the boxes through the garage and stacked in the corner of the kitchen. Heavier than I thought, I was tired, so I rested in the chair next to our bed while Ric napped watching *Jeopardy* and doing my best to swallow spoonsful of a somewhat tasteless canned soup I found in the pantry.

Once he was situated for the night, I took my shower, dried my hair, and got ready for bed. Ricardo looked comfortable, and I was so delighted to have him back home lying next to me. I set my alarm for 2:00 a.m. That was two hours from the time I closed my eyes and drifted off. When my alarm rang, notifying me it was time to get up and fix his pump, I was groggy. Ric stayed asleep. I was back in bed by 2:20 a.m. with the alarm now set for 5:00 a.m. This time it wasn't as easy to fall asleep. I was without question exhausted, but it was close to the time I would normally wake up with Ric before he was admitted.

I lay in bed under the thick down quilts wondering if God had been speaking to me since I was a child. Pondering the pain, I have suffered sense childhood. Was it only to help me live my true purpose? I have read many versions of the Bible, many times. That night, Ephesians 2:10 flashed through my mind. That verse meant that we should do the work that God assigned us to do.

Wanting us to make good on the talent he gave us or the purpose that came from our pain? I contemplated whether our talent and our purpose are the same thing until the alarm rang again.

> For we are his workmanship created in Christ Jesus unto good works which God hath before ordained that we should walk in them.
>
> —Ephesians 2:10 (KJV)

This time Ric was up; he wanted to go to the bathroom, he also wanted some ice chips. Ice and hard candies like lemon drops were the only things he could consume.

"Do you remember that flavored ice we had in Hawaii. What was that called."

I paused for a moment to think about it. "Shaved ice."

"Wow, I would love some shaved ice."

I grabbed my phone; there it was on Amazon. An entire shaved ice kit including six flavors, the machine, and white plastic-coated paper cones to fill up. I added it to my cart along with a can of traditional old-fashioned hard candies. I clicked buy now and fell asleep.

There was so much I didn't comprehend. What was my purpose? Why did I have to be doing this all over again caring for another man I loved, watching him deteriorate right before my eyes? Grief makes us see things differently, and I was already grieving the loss of the life I had only a month ago. I could see Ricardo, face rounder, fuller, sitting on the bright royal blue bench somewhere in Kona holding a cone of blue shaved ice with his jovial, heartwarming smile peeking out from under the tan baseball cap we purchased about sixty miles away on the other side of the island. With all my heart I wanted to believe we would be there together again, on the Big Island, Oahu, Maui, and Kauai too. I wanted to believe in one of God's miracles. I knew God created us all as intelligent beings. He gave us the ability to heal ourselves, to create medicines that helped us, and to have doctors for that purpose as well. They were how he created some of his miracles.

> And lest I should be exalted above measure through the abundance of the revelations, there was given to me a thorn in the flesh, the messenger of Satan to buffet me, lest I should be exalted above measure.
>
> —2 Corinthians 12:7 (KJV)

I also understood that not everyone is made whole again. Although Paul did not get healed, God gave him the strength to bear the pain of his infliction as is evident in 2 Corinthians 12:7 Although some scholars refer to the thorn as hardship and not sickness, believing sickness is never God's will for our lives. Why then are some of God's children struck with disease? Other scholars claim Paul's malady was epilepsy considering revelations could be visions that commonly accompany seizures, which are consistent with the disease. Debating scripture is not helpful for us today. Making some sense of the suffering in the world, our own pain, grief—these need to be addressed for our hearts to heal. What we need to see is how God works through suffering to call us closer to him.

The real question is what do we do with that pain? On July 27, 1981, a six-year-old boy was abducted from a shopping mall in Hollywood Florida. The fear of having your child go missing must be horrific. The only thing that I can imagine must be worse is to have that missing child found dead. That's what happened to John Walsh. From this pain came his purpose. Mr. Walsh went on to start a television show called *America's Most Wanted*. This show helped catch over one thousand fugitives. If

John Walsh never lost his son to such a tragic situation, would he have been able to do what he did?

Let me be clear. I am not justifying the death of his son, but if he did not suffer through that pain, he would not have found such a purposeful passion. God was trying to tell me what I should do with my pain, I couldn't understand it all. When we are broken, when we can't see a light in front of us and when we don't know how we can go on, God speaks to us. But we don't always listen to what he is telling us. When our kids don't listen to us, what do we do? We speak firmer, we get louder, we may even be forced to yell. What does our father God do when we don't listen to what he is telling us? He tells us again but the second time it's louder and clearer.

> Behold, what manner of love the Father hath bestowed upon us, that we should be called the sons of God: therefore, the world knoweth us not, because it knew him not.
>
> —1 John 3:1 (KJV)

I ask you to stop a moment and investigate ways God showed himself to you. This may be difficult, and perhaps you can't see a way that he has just yet. That's okay too. If not, remember that every day there is beauty around you even when death is there too. Try to write down a few things surrounding you that are beautiful. It could be the love of family, that call or visit from a friend, or it could be as simple as a beautiful flower in full bloom.

_____

_____

_____

_____

> Neither do men light a candle, and put it under a bushel, but on a candlestick; and it giveth light unto all that are in the house. Let your light so shine before men, that they may see your good works, and glorify your Father which is in heaven.
>
> —Matthew 5:15–16 (KJV)

The first day posed challenges. A nurse came from the Cape Cod Nurses Association to help me get Ricardo situated. I was surprised when the doorbell rang. She used all the clean towels in our linen closet, soiled the bedsheets, and left Ricardo sitting up uncomfortably by the side of the bed. After I cleaned up from her visit and got my husband comfortably to bed, the phone rang notifying me of her visit. Do everything in the house, help my daughter, Tagan, with her home schooling, manage my studio—it was overwhelming. God gave me the strength I needed and the revelation that he would reveal his purpose to me in time.

8

TESTS

> Then they cry unto the Lord in their trouble, and he
> saveth them out of their distress.
>
> —Psalm 107:19 (KJV)

Monotonous days are sometimes glorious. I came to this realization after a few weeks of Ricardo's return home. There was a calm tranquility in my new routine. But Thanksgiving was approaching, and family members threatened to visit. Normally I would love the excitement of decorating, cooking, and entertaining. However, Ricardo's cancer diagnosis had changed us. Pragmatically speaking, we could not do any of those things because cooking meats and other food with strong scent caused Ricardo to vomit. He could not afford this, as he needed all the calories he could consume. He returned home from BWH eighty pounds lighter than the spring before his diagnosis. His weight was declining. Scheduled for chemo the Friday after Thanksgiving, I needed to keep his strength up. Personally, I did not have the strength to be festive.

Selfishly, I wanted that Thanksgiving to be mine: sitting next to the bed watching the parade on TV, some football after, perhaps a walk to the pond if he felt up to it followed by a nap. I didn't need the turkey or all the fixings, and I was understanding that Thanksgiving should be every day. I was also realizing that, although most likely the Pilgrims did sit down with the Wompanoag tribe after a successful harvest of corn about thirty miles from our home in November of 1621. The peace did not last between them, and in some sense the holiday is only a reminder of the oppression the natives had to withstand.

Against my better judgment, I foolishly permitted visitors into our home. That night while Ric napped, I opened a bottle of wine and told them how worried I was and how we could not cook anything the next day. I requested that they eat the pastry I purchased for breakfast and enjoy some conversation before going off to a local restaurant with my daughter for the traditional dinner. They agreed. Then they asked questions—how was he doing, his prognosis, his mental capacity?

Then the big one — "Why wasn't Ricardo diagnosed earlier?"

Unable to express that my husband went to the doctor over fifteen times, and there really wasn't anything else I could have done. I was washed with blame all over again. Did you blame yourself for something you had no control over? This is a normal feeling associated with grief. Please take a moment to say this short prayer:

Father God,

Please bring comfort to me.

Let me understand that I do not have the power to change the past.

Favor me with the courage to accept the circumstances around me.

And the strength to overcome the difficulties that face me today.

Amen

There is so much power in prayer, just as in realizing that there are things in life that we cannot change, that we don't have the power to stop, and that can be one of our most difficult lessons. Growing up I thought everything was my fault. When my grandfather passed away after being ill for approximately fourteen years, my mom intimated that he died because I broke his heart. That guilt became a constant companion through most of my life. When my first husband died, I was stricken with that guilt once again. Even though the doctors kept telling me he only had "two more months," every eight weeks I was certain I caused him to pass. Truthfully, at times the last day of his life still haunts me. He was supposed to be released from the hospital. The night before, I had left his room to retrieve a ginger ale he had requested. Tired, I didn't notice the floors were slippery and wet. I slid down on my back, and the accident triggered an anxiety attack. I was rushed downstairs to the emergency room just as I had been with the flu at BWH. They kept me overnight with an oxygen mask strapped to my face and an intravenous needle jabbed into my vein.

I was still weak the next morning, the nurses offered to wash him before the ambulance came for him, which was a godsend. He refused. I overrode his decision. I just wouldn't have had the strength to wash him up at home. The minute the nurse rolled him over, he began gasping for breath. Before I understood what was happening, they called for morphine. Eight hours in a coma was all we had left.

I never left his side, just sat there with our fingers locked together until I felt the life leave his hand as Alex Trebek enthusiastically announced it was time for Double Jeopardy. For months I believed if only I had not insisted on the bath, he would have not passed. Of course, that was not true.

Ricardo was my attorney; we became friends first and that friendship developed into something deeper. We were "battle buddies." Eventually we started dating. There is no accidental meeting of souls. God's plans are set. Ricardo was the one that taught me that, made me realize I was powerless. That feeling is both liberating and scary. I won't lie and say that the guilt doesn't creep back in every now and again. I told you I went to Catholic School, and Catholic guilt does exist.

Thanksgiving morning, I woke up before the 8:00 a.m. alarm to Ricardo slumped over the side of the bed vomiting, the scent of homemade pancakes and bacon wafting into our room. Our guests had awakened early, and even though I had been clear about food the night before, they decided they wanted a warm, hearty breakfast. He was never able to get out of bed that day.

Continually checking to make sure the area around the tubes in his stomach was clean and dry was another daily task. Repeatedly watching for infection in that tender and runny area was important. Something else to worry about. In addition, draining the bile from the j-tube also included recording the amounts that were being collected. The next day, I would have to report the number had not gone down.

He was weak, and I needed to stay close by when he would want to get up and go to the bathroom. Our company found a restaurant serving the traditional turkey, stuffing, and all the other fixings. They went out. His brothers drove up from Rhode Island and mounted a brand-new TV on the wall in the bedroom; a friend installed a higher toilet seat to make it easier. There was a lot to be grateful for.

Chemo was scheduled for 8:30 a.m. We left the house at five forty-five the day after that Thanksgiving. We both looked forward to that appointment, holding every hope that the drug would be the magic pill. The ride to Boston was uneventful; we talked about politics, about Tagan getting a math tutor, and we held hands while I drove. We arrived early.

The registration process seemed confusing; it required us going to visit various floors of Dana Faber. After the blood work, we waited, thinking we were going to meet a new doctor. I didn't really understand what happened but a heavyset nurse in blue scrubs called us in to a long corridor; she asked how he was feeling. I tried to tell her about the infection on his abdomen, but before I could say anything else, she had sat Ric down in a wheelchair and was quickly pushing him through long corridors. I briskly walked behind them carrying both our winter coats, my purse, my heavy bookbag, and his backpack that his brother Mark gave him filled with cans of feed, a bottle of water, lip balm, his wallet, medical cards, and a charger. It was that day that I realized Dana Faber Cancer Centre was attached to Brigham and Women's Hospital. Somehow, we had walked right by the cafeteria I vomited in, and we were boarding the elevator down to the emergency room I was brought to.

It sounds like one of those #inspiration posts on Instagram, but it is true. The only constant in our life was change. I always see that comment posted on social media because it is true. God cannot allow us to stay comfortable for too long, especially if he needs us to live our purpose. That's why he doesn't just let us travel our journey in a smooth, straight line. I just never would have believed how unrecognizable my life could get. How bumpy the road could be?

I already confessed how my gut instinct told me something wasn't right before he was diagnosed. When he would be late getting home after work, I worried his car had gone off the side of the road. When my phone rang, and I didn't recognize the number, my head would possess all kinds of crazy thoughts. I never thought it would be cancer and now that it was, I had this gnawing deep inside that just like Nuno, we wouldn't make it past that ten-year anniversary. Miracles can happen, I was praying. However, if I listened to his doctors, the miracle would be to have one more Christmas together. Ricardo was being admitted to BWH again.

I knew all too well nothing could last forever, but the day we had walked down the aisle, I was convinced I had found the man I would grow old with. Like I said earlier, we were coming up on our ten-year anniversary just like with my first husband. I was aware of how difficult it was for me. I couldn't even fathom what he must have felt. To have a doctor look at you and tell you there was a deadly disease inside your body and, statistically, you don't have a fighting chance. My first husband, Nuno, and my dad had to have heard those words as well. How did they process hearing that? Why did all the men I loved have to suffer this way? Of course, they were angry, scared, confused.

They say when we write, we write about what we know. As you see, this memoir reveals that grief is something I understand, and writing does help us. I started writing right after my dad passed away. I have kept a diary since I was eight. It has helped me remember my loss and my pain and my love. I do not really think of myself as a writer; I'm just a Christian with a story.

I urge you to get a lined notebook, perhaps one with a picture on the cover that you find enticing or beautiful. This will help you to want to pick it up and use it more often. Keep it somewhere that will be convenient:

1. On your nightstand if you think you will use it when you first wake up or before falling asleep.
2. In your kitchen if you feel you may write while you have your morning coffee or tea.
3. By a favorite chair you sit and relax in regularly.

You don't have to write a lot. One word can be enough some days. Others you may want to write pages recounting a memory that makes you smile. There are no rules. You may want to record a favorite scripture in one entry. Writing is a practice that offers help when we are grieving, but that may not be for you. Think about drawing, scrapbooking, or journaling. Try to find something that helps you reflect on your loved one, your emotions, and your way of coping.

I knew he was frail; I knew he had been throwing up Thanksgiving morning. He had been anxious; we both were. I got all dressed up that morning in my blue skirt that had a print of blooming beige dahlias that coordinated perfectly with the beige sweater I had purchased at Lord and Taylor last winter. Heels and purse matched as well. It was going to be a big day.

It was going to be his first chemo appointment, and we truly were filled with promise. From the time I got him out of the car and up to the laboratory at Dana Faber to the end of the night when I finally was back in my car driving home alone was a mirage of unexpected events. I still couldn't really process what had happened. The next morning, I woke up in my bed still in the clothes I had worn. Wanting to call Ric, I grabbed my phone and noticed a Facebook post that went something like this:

> To all my Facebook friends and family
> I regret to inform you I have Stage IV stomach cancer
> I have been in the hospital from the beginning of October
> Unfortunately, they were unable to remove my tumor
> I have been on a feeding tube since October 13
> I have a drain for my stomach
> This is the most trying time in my life
> I was back home for a brief time
> I would love a card or text
> I was scheduled to begin Chemo
> But I had a set back with a life-threatening complication
> My sodium levels are so low I am back in the hospital
> They need to regulate this
> I am a fighter
> This cancer was caused by my service in the USMC
> I was stationed at Camp Lejeune NC 37 years ago
> The water was poisoned by the constant dumping of chemicals from a dry-cleaning facility on base
> It was a cancer-causing nightmare
> I served there from October 1975 to February 1977
> I was Marine of the month for my regime for three months in a row
> It seems so unfair but so isn't life if you really think about it
> I will pursue a 100% disability claim

To close out I saw my primary care physician 15 times since
last March
He repeatedly told me it was heartburn or Gerd
It is a bitter pill to swallow
Please pray for me

Crying is one thing; wailing is altogether different. I read it
repeatedly as I sat in bed uttering a high-pitched, prolonged, and
mournful cry. The post had already gotten over fifty likes and
loves. He needed to write it down to express his fear and anger.
He was processing, coping, and grieving as well.

9

CHRISTMAS

> A merry heart doeth good like medicine: but a broken
> spirit drieth the bones.
>
> —Proverbs 17:22 (KJV)

God is great. *By a stroke of insightful genius, Dr. Clancy* figured out that Ricardo needed saline to combat a potential stroke, brain damage, or worst, death. He was coming home for Christmas, and I was overjoyed to be able to pick him up and bring him back to our house on Cape Cod. Making it even better, Ricardo believed his travails would help others, through his situation it was discovered that saline added to his bag instead of regular water helped. Would all patients battling stomach cancer that were on a pump benefit from this?

Ricardo posted a poem by Amy Willowroot:

> May my path be blessed, as I walk into the future.
> May my footsteps be of benefit to others.
> I am one, may my journey be joyous.

Certain days, tears help. That day was one of those days. I stood in my kitchen looking out on the frozen ground crying. I had put my trust in God, and he was responding to my daily prayer. I believed that he would take care of me; he would give me the strength I needed, and as time passed, he would reveal his purpose. I was grateful for it all—the saline discovery that stabilized his sodium level. Thankful Ricardo was coming home again—but for God. The doctors were making miracles; he was gaining a bit of strength, and I had been able to visit every day. The blessings of this beautiful season were many. It was Christmas, and although I had not decorated the house as I normally would, I had a small fresh tree in the family room that filled the downstairs with the fresh scent of balsam fir. Santas were festively placed around and complemented the sparkle and shine from just enough gold and silver ornaments and ribbon that I was able to carry up from the basement to cover the little tree that I proudly carried in from the top of the SABB all by myself. Ric would see it today. He would be home for Christmas, so why was I crying? I needed that cry to cleanse my soul.

Crying can bring comfort to us. It is a natural response to an array of emotions, not just sadness and grief. Suppressing your tears is not healthy. When we allow ourselves to cry, we are reducing our own distress, calming ourselves down, and regulating our thoughts because crying activates the parasympathetic nervous system. Some research indicates that crying relieves stress. If you feel like you want or need to cry, it's okay. Allow yourself the time and space to do so.

Those tears helped me. The stress I was holding was gone. I was able to get myself together and make my way to Boston—stopping at the Braintree Mall to buy some new clothes for Ricardo on the way. He had lost so much weight that nothing fit him properly anymore. The gray polo sweatsuit I purchased at Macy's with the zip up jacket brought a smile to his face.

"I think I still look kind of handsome."

"Babe, you are without question as handsome as you were the day, I married you." I kissed him on the lips.

For the first time in a long time, that interaction felt intimate. The kiss was sensual in the way we used to be. The way a man kisses his wife. I had been so busy being his caregiver I forgot how much I missed being his lover.

Two nights after Ricardo was home, he mentioned guests stopping by. He requested homemade hot chocolate, the kind that contains only pure cocoa, whole milk, sugar, and salt. Of course, I made sure that the Christmas staple would be accompanied by a large platter of sugar cookies.

"Make sure you put out our best cups, all twelve of them out."

Twelve! I couldn't figure out who was coming, and he didn't want to tell me either. At six o' clock, he was up on the couch in the living room wearing the new green PJ's I had gotten him when he first came home from the hospital. Hair combed and clean shaven with a hint of cologne, I could see the anticipation on his face. Fifteen minutes past six, the doorbell chimed. A balding man with kind eyes in a brown leather jacket stood on my front step. Behind him, lined along the walkway, were seven women and two other men, all holding song books. When I pulled open the door, they began singing "Jingle Bells," as I instinctively welcomed them in. It was wonderful to witness. Like a good holiday movie, I felt warm and fuzzy inside. They sang several songs. But the true gift was when they all stood in a circle around the couch my husband was resting on, and with strong, beautiful voices intricately woven together began a hymn:

Hark! The herald angels sing,
"Glory to the newborn King!
Peace on earth and mercy mild,
God and sinners reconciled."
Joyful, all ye nations rise,
Join the triumph of the skies,
With th' angelic host proclaim:
"Christ is born in Bethlehem."
Hark! The herald angels sing,
"Glory to the newborn King!"

It was so moving; Ric had tears in his eyes, and so did I. Through those tears filled with hope, we looked deep into each other's souls. It was as if he were telling me he was scared; he didn't want to leave; he wasn't ready, and I was silently telling him I wasn't either, but I would be there for him no matter what. It was a night I will never forget. That beautiful carol based on Luke 2:14 will always be my favorite Christmas song.

Afterward, I served the hot chocolate and cookies to our

carolers. As it turned out, the leader of this amazing group knew Ric. Several years ago, his wife had lost her teenage daughter. Ricardo helped her through that horrific time. There are widows and orphans, but no words can describe a mother who grieves her child.

Christmas Eve, a few nights later, which was usually spent at his brother's home, would be different. We were not going to be able to make that family gathering all the way down to Rhode Island. Tagan was disappointed, but it was just too much. Instead, we would celebrate at home. We invited friends; my daughter had met Bella in swimming class at the YMCA when they were both in preschool. Instantly they connected, and I became friends with her mom, Ric with her dad. Our two families enjoyed many a night together at each other's houses. We were all looking forward to the get-together. I had turned on the lights, and we eagerly waited for them to pull into the driveway.

Instead, I saw the UPS truck drive up. A padded manila envelope addressed to Ricardo M. Barros was left at the door. I retrieved the package and handed it to my husband.

"Babe, something came for you."

He had a mischievous look in his eye. "You didn't think I would forget your present this year, did you?" He smiled, and just like always, when he did his entire face beamed. "It's for you, my beautiful wife."

Inside was a magnificent crucifix in two-tone yellow and white 14 karat gold. The cross hung on a delicate figaro chain that complemented the piece perfectly. It was stunning. Once again, I was brought to tears as Ric placed it around my neck. I never wanted to take it off.

The entire night was magical. We talked, laughed, and listened to music. It was a celebration of life. I had set out cheese and crackers, strawberries, and grapes for us to nibble on. I had opened a couple of bottles of wine as well. Throwing caution to the wind, I poured myself a glass while we waited for Chinese food to be delivered, then another while I ate my Singapore rice noodles. Those few hours everything seemed like it always was. I had one more glass of merlot. None of us wanted the night to end, Ric was getting tired. We all said the customary "Merry Christmas," and it was time to get ready for bed.

The wine made me tired. I had put on warm flannel pajamas and got my husband comfortable in bed. I administered the pain meds and the newly prescribed sleeping pills. As I filled his bag with formula and a syringe up with saline ready to flush into his tube, the liquid came spitting back out at me. I was confused, and Ric was groggy. It took several times before I realized there was a blockage in his tube. After contacting the on-call doctor, I was told I had to get him to the BWH emergency room. My nerves kicked in; hastily I threw on a gray turtleneck and my jeans. Getting Ricardo into the car was a challenge, staying alert on the dark, empty route to Boston was even more challenging.

The emergency room was filled with people—a little girl crying and holding her arm that was most likely broken, a woman clenching her stomach and screaming, an old couple with no apparent symptoms, and a young man with flushed skin barely breathing. He was covered with sores and scabs; his eyes were puffy and dark. A few other nondescript individuals were dispersed around the large waiting area. After giving Ric's medical information, I was certain we would be brought in immediately. Surely the admittance nurse would realize Ricardo's condition demanded urgent care. Instead, we were told to take a seat with everyone else.

The night was long and stressful. I was exhausted and ended up falling asleep on a hospital bed. Ricardo posted a picture of me curled up on the bed still in my plaid coat with the big fur collar we bought up in North Conway the previous winter on a ski trip. I was sound asleep, the railings of the bed raised so that I wouldn't roll over. The post was on Facebook for everyone to see:

> Had a big adventure last night. We had a party. They ordered Chinese (which of course I couldn't eat.) We watched my early Christmas gift, The complete *Star Wars*. At 10:30 I took my sleeping pill got ready for bed then my feeding tube blocked. No matter what we could not unblock it. We had to go to the Brigham's emergency room on Christmas Eve. Bummer. I felt bad for my loyal, dedicated loving wife Sabrina who ended up sleeping in a hospital bed until 7 am Christmas Day when we finally got to leave. Arriving back on Cape at 9 am Christmas morning, once again Dr. Clancy's team came to my aid. I was exceptionally concerned about getting the salinity to maintain my sodium level so as not to be back in the hospital for another week. It was shaping up to be 12 hours without food or water. I kept trying to get them to hang a bag of saline. They were not listening to me. I began to be afraid of effects of not having the saline water. I finally decided to pray to God for help. I asked him to send my patron Saint Michael the patron saint of warriors to come and help these people understand that I needed the water. I just finished the prayer as in 3 seconds when the curtain opened, and nurse Olivia Parsons said I don't care what the doctor says I'm hanging the saline because you need it now. She was a little angel. God immediately answered my request for help. If Sabrina were not present, who would believe me? A Christmas

Miracle. God is with me always. His Rod and his
staff comfort me. I am going to beat this because
he is always at my side. Merry Christmas and
Happy New Year. Don't be afraid to ask for help
he will hear you.

He had indeed heard our prayers; not only had the nurse
administered the Saline Ric was so concerned about, but she
was able to use a long thin metal rod, which she used to gently
push the hardened formula through the tube without tearing
it. We were back home for Christmas with our daughter and
family. It was a beautiful day. That night, I prayed it would not
be our last Christmas together.

Take a moment to remember a special moment during a
celebration that you spent with your loved one. It could be
heartfelt or lighthearted. Jot it down in your journal, and as
that time of year rolls around, share that memory with a family
member or friend.

_____

_____

_____

_____

10

HIBERNATION

C hristmas was over; all the sparkling lights, fragile glass balls, and elegantly dressed Santa Clauses were neatly packed away—strategically placed on wood shelves in our cluttered basement eagerly awaiting the next year. Outside, the cold hard soil waited for the first blanket of snow to fall while the trees were already wearing spring bulbs patiently waiting to burst into bloom. Most people were in that waiting period. I, however, was content in the hibernation of winter. Everything somehow seemed to be normal, routine now. I was comfortable in my warm cluttered house with Ricardo and Tagan. I rarely went to my studio before 9:00 a.m., which was somewhat blissful. Every morning I would make two cups of piping hot coffee and carefully carry them back into the bedroom. Our two Siberian cats, now sporting their thick winter coats, would accompany me. Ricardo would sit up, which he was able to do on his own, and I would retreat to the hard-red wingback chair that seemed so comfortable. The four of us would watch the news, which seemed to be equally exciting and aggravating due to the crazy election that would be held in ten months. I would drink my coffee black and strong, quickly, then run back into the kitchen for a refill. My husband, carefully circling his spoon around inside his mug that we bought on our trip to Alaska, would smile and say, "I think I had enough," without even lifting it to his lips.

After changing his feed, draining his bag, and administering his medicine, I would get myself ready for work. Wearing my long, thick, black coat with the fur-trim hood that would never stay on and my red knit hat with the ear flaps, I looked more like a Canadian then a Cape Coder. Somehow, being on time seemed impossible to me. My clients were always parked outside my studio waiting for me to pull in. They slowly started dropping off. I didn't really notice until my bank statements started showing the decline in income. My studio was my constant, a big part of my life. I had opened it with my first husband,

and between private clients and group classes, I would usually teach forty hours a week. I loved it. Early-morning mat classes, followed by privates on my Pilates or Gyrotonic equipment, another regular 5:30 p.m. group class followed by a ballet class. I always felt like I made a difference in my clients' lives. I had people with Parkinson's, stroke victims, people with muscular dystrophy, multiple sclerosis, Ehlers-Danlos syndrome, women who needed that burn, and stunning young teens who aspired to dance in a major ballet company. But I didn't want to teach or coach, I didn't even want to work out. Thinner than I had been in years, I didn't look healthy or strong. Instead, I looked exhausted, frazzled, and not at all present. After a couple of private seasons, I would retreat home.

Tagan would have walked the dog, checked on her dad, and be seated at the kitchen counter blankly looking at her schoolwork I had left for her the night before when I would return. By then, the bag would need to be drained and a few more cans of liquid would need to be added into Ricardo's pump. I would get him up and washed. We would make it to the family room where Ric would sit carefully on the long burgundy couch, which was the same couch that I would cuddle up with my dad on during the long winter months when I was just a young girl. It was my dad's favorite season—I think partly because it reminded him of Sweden and partly because he loved the colors—evergreen, berry red, frosty gray, and the orchid that flashed across the stark winter sky. Winter with a furry blanket, a warm cup of tea, and a good book always reminded me of my youth, my father, and thoughts of how different I would be had he lived long enough to help raise me.

The winter days sitting sandwiched between Ricardo and the side table stacked with an array of books comprised of Scandinavian mysteries, a biography or two, a cookbook from some faraway country, and my Bible, all of which I had

difficulty reading, were filled with quite different thoughts.
Dark thoughts that I tried to push away. I had already been
a widow once before. I had experienced the fear of being left
alone to handle it all, the loneliness of no longer having the
one person you are most intimate with next to you, the anger,
the shock, the confusion. I didn't know if I could do it again. I
didn't know if I would be in the midst of trying to do it again
next winter.

I wondered what Ricardo thought. He never told me he
was afraid. He stayed positive and believed that God would
heal him. Tagan as well, what was running through her mind?
Knowing her biological father had died of stage IV cancer
and now watching her dad, the only dad she knew, battle this
horrible disease must have been horrifying for her. She never
spoke about it either. Every afternoon all those same questions
would dance in my mind until it was time to make something
to eat. Ricardo would go back to bed most afternoons, but
there were a few special days when he would feel well enough
to sit at the counter with Tagan as I cooked—helping her with
schoolwork and offering some tips for whatever it was I was
making. I savored those days. Then the pump would need my
attention, pills would need to be administered, and then I would
force myself back to the studio for a couple more hours. Every
day was just like the one before, and I absolutely loved the
routine, the new normal because it included Ricardo.

We talked about that trip to Hawaii, adopting a new kitten;
we would make election predications and lists of food we needed
to buy even though Ric couldn't eat, and I barely could either.
When I got home, I would clean up, go over Tagan's work, and
set out everything for the next day—more meds, the pump, a
little TV—and then sleep for three full hours until my alarm
would ring so I could get back up, drain the bag, and refill the
pump again. As I said, every day except for Wednesdays when
we would have to get up early for chemo.

A part of me was in denial. Realistically, I knew Ricardo couldn't live with stage IV stomach cancer, tubes protruding from his abdomen, pain, and pills for years on end. I couldn't continue my schedule the way it was—lack of sleep, lack of nourishment, lack of exercise. I would deteriorate as well. But in that season, I was grateful.

Wednesdays were a gift, a time for us to get dressed up and venture out. We would drive along Route 6 crossing over the Sagamore Bridge passing over the Saltonstall Bikeway across the Cape Cod Canal. It seemed like a different lifetime when we would ride the bikeway as a family. Ricardo and Tagan would always race ahead of me; I would trail behind using the excuse that I was just soaking in the beauty of the canal, but in reality, my knees would start to ache, and it would slow me down. Each week Ricardo would talk about the coming summer and riding along the canal again. God knew how hard I prayed for that to happen along with all the other amazing summer activities that once seemed ordinary and now I would consider gifts. We would stop at Mary-Lou's, and I would get two coffees and gas up. From Sagamore to Rockland there was hardly any traffic, but from Hingham all the way into Boston there was a lot of traffic to navigate. We would crawl past the rainbow swash each week. A gas tank that somehow became Boston's most controversial artwork. The bright burst of color was painted by a Catholic nun in the early 1970s. The rainbow is a bright composition of orange, yellow, red, blue, green, and purple. The splash of blue resembles a face with a pointy goatee much like the one Ho Chi Minh wore. The landmark always prompted intellectual conversation that stimulated both of us until we found our way to the dark, congested garage under Dana Faber.

Unspoken prayers were said by both of us as we rode the elevator up to the fifth floor. We both understood that his red blood cells, white blood cells, and platelets had to be exactly

right for chemo to be administered. Chemo was our hope. We
clung to the belief that if Dr. Enzinger gave the thumbs-up, there
was a chance for healing, for wholeness. I would use the time
that Ricardo was getting chemo to close my eyes and rest, to
read my Bible, to meditate on scripture.

> Shew me thy way, O Lord; teach me thy path.
>
> Lead me in thy truth, and teach me: for thou art the God
> of my salvation; On thee do I wait all the day.
>
> —Psalm 25: 4–5 (KJV)

Many of you may have experienced similar situations. The
role of the care giver is not easy. If you are currently taking
care of a terminally ill loved one. remember you need to first
take care of yourself so you can continue providing the level of
care required. If you are now grieving the loss of a spouse, even
a parent, child, other family member or friend that you cared
for, you may be experiencing changes in your body. If your
loss was sudden, it can still take a toll out on you physically
and mentally. You may have gained weight or lost it. You may
have developed aches and pains in your back or neck. Loss
manifests in our body just as it does in our heart and head. The
heartbreak of grief can raise blood pressure, create heart issues,
increase inflammation, it can beat up your immune system and
aggravate health challenges you already have. Sleep may be
challenging; you may sleep all day and be up all night; you may
lay restless for nights on end and barely function during the day.
You need to start to take care of yourself. Exercise is medicine
for your body as well as for your mind.

Physical activity builds your mental state up by releasing
endorphins. Grief is not depression, but it can lead to it quickly.
Exercise will help combat that as well as fight some of the body

aches and pains from increasing. Start slow—fifteen minutes a day can make a significant difference. Walking, Pilates, swimming are great low-impact exercises if you are not up to joining a group class. But if you are, getting out and being around other people is a great motivation.

11

LISTS

The ground was thawing, the sun was setting later in the day, and spring with the promise of new life had snuck up on us. For the first time, I was sad to see winter leave. I would have been happy frozen in that season, secure that nothing would get worse or, for that matter, better. That everything could just stay as it was—comfortable. Nature has a way of allowing us to cope with our lives, sometimes forcing us to live. The shorter days of those cold months allowed me to rest up—hibernate. Now I had to brace myself for an entire new season.

Ricardo was excited about the promise of spring. He was making a list, perhaps a bucket list of sorts. All the things he wanted us to do:

> A trip to Niagara Falls
> A trip to the Bay of Fundy
> A new boat
> Adopting a new kitten
> A Broadway performance
> The symphony
> Hawaii (next winter)

He told everybody as if saying his goals aloud would help them to manifest. I wanted so badly to make him happy, to fulfill his every wish, that I immediately decided I would start figuring out ways to check each item off the list. Boston's Symphony Hall is a truly magnificent building. It is considered one of the top concert halls in the world, and although I had never been inside, I knew it would be breathtaking. I jumped on the website and immediately noticed tickets for Joshua Bell with the Academy of Saint Martin in the Fields. One of his younger brothers was a huge help to me. Mark had a daughter only a year younger than Tagan. How perfect; the five of us would have a special experience that we would all remember forever. Ricardo was delighted to listen to the world-class violinist play such varied music from tender, refined, vulnerable emotion to strong, robust, powerful beauty. It was a moving Sunday afternoon for us both. The picture of me in my black cashmere with the gold cross hanging from my neck next to my handsome husband dressed in his newly tailored gray wool suit will always be in my heart. The picture of the girls and Mark gently nodding off also lingers. I'm not sure that they enjoyed the concert, but it was impossible not to relish in the delight Ric experienced.

You may not have gone to the symphony, but there were times that meant something to you that you shared with your loved one. There is power in these memories. The word is nostalgic. Take a moment to make a list of five happy memories. It could just be a simple meal you shared together that you both enjoyed. It could be a social interaction you had as a couple. A memory you look back on that you are grateful for.

1._____

2._____

3._____

4._____

5._____

When we are stressed, grieving, and hurt, recalling positive, joyful experiences help us to combat sadness. The stories we tell ourselves and other people are ways we can recall memories that fill our heads and hearts with positivity instead of negative pathways. Try to share each memory with a different person. Call a friend and just simply ask, "Can I tell you about the time ..."

Sometimes these events that we shared with our loved one can trigger an anniversary reaction. This is normal and can continue for years after the loss. It can cause anger, tears, guilt, pain, depression, and anxiety. You may have trouble sleeping as it gets close to the time of year that you shared a special moment. To combat this, you may want to consider planning a special event with your child, a friend, or family member. For example, if the anniversary of that day at the symphony becomes a lot for me, I could turn it into a healing opportunity by planning a concert or special dinner with my daughter. In other words, create a new tradition or a distraction. Just know that grief is unpredictable, and you are entitled to feel a range of emotions from tears to laughter.

Now make a list of five things you have always wanted to do for yourself, places you have wanted to go, or something special you have wanted to purchase. It's okay to make plans, travel, redecorate, or buy a new car:

1._____

2._____

3._____

4._____

5._____

That Wednesday back at Dana Faber, we got some incredible news. Ricardo had gained weight and was now at a healthy 175 pounds. He was cleared to start eating eggs, cheese, soup, and small meals that included meat if they were blended in the Vitamix. This was wonderful, and Ric was so excited. The best part of our day was learning that but for God his tumor had shrunk. In addition, my diligence in tracking bile showed the drain in his stomach was not producing as much. Doctor

Enzinger looked at us, and for the first time, I could see the faint sign of a smile.

He crossed his legs. "Mr. Barros, you're doing good."

"I reverently pray to the great healer, and he is powerful."

I could tell Dr. Enzinger was a man of science. That is not to say he didn't have faith, but he was about the "how," not the "why," and he was about the business of medicine. I was certain if asked he would say religion and science are incompatible, but it didn't matter at that moment.

He paused, as though processing what my husband had said. Maybe I was wrong. Then he ran his hand through his thick brown hair. "Hmm, well, ah, if you keep it up there is no reason why we can't consider having both the tubes removed."

I was ecstatic; there was hope. The doctor was scheduling a cat scan to see if the tumor may have shrunk. There was something to thank God for and something new to pray for. It was a fourteen-hour day from the time we left the Cape to the time we returned home. We saw the doctor; Ricardo got labs and his chemo. We ate lunch in the cafeteria, and throughout the day, Ric shared the memory of Joshua Bell and Symphony Hall with everyone he encountered.

The following Tuesday was his cat scan; I sat next to him in a big orange chair looking at a gardening magazine patiently waiting for them to call Barros. I didn't realize my mobile ringer was on until it rang loudly. Without even looking at the incoming number, I picked it up.

"Hello."

The man on the other end started talking in a formal British accent just as the nurse stepped out from a small room off the side of the waiting are with a folder in her hands. "Mr. Barros."

I didn't know what to do. I wanted to go in with Ricardo, but I had to stay on the line. My first husband's brother had passed away in Portugal. The funeral was in two days, and his son-in-law was asking me to attend with my daughter.

> We are troubled on every side, yet not distressed: we
> are perplexed, but not in despair.
>
> —2 Corinthians 4:8 (KJV)

We arrived home from the cat scan at 11:30 a.m. I immediately secured two tickets from Boston's Logan Airport to Lisbon, a direct flight on Trans Air Portugal leaving at eight o'clock that same evening. Ricardo asked his brother to stay with him while we were away—a total of three and a half days. I nervously told Tagan what happened and to pack a bag. We were heading to Lisbon.

Learning of Carlos's passing conjured memories of my first husband. The way he would bite his bottom lip when he felt mischievous and how he would cock his head to the left whenever he was annoyed. Nuno was older than me by over twenty years. I know that can be shocking. Handsome, sophisticated, and debonair, I met him right before my twenty-first birthday. It wasn't love at first sight although I thought he was very attractive, well dressed, and interesting. He was my friend; he was kind and protective in a fatherly way. Maybe I needed that at the time. Our first date wasn't supposed to be a date at all. We were simply talking about food—Indian food. I loved saag paneer, tandoori, jalfrezi, and a few other dishes. He told me he always wanted to try it and nonchalantly asked me if I wanted to go with him. I agreed. He picked me up in a three-piece Italian silk suit, had flowers in his hand, and smelled of expensive cologne and tobacco. We never ended up at the casual little Indian spot I had originally recommended. Instead, we found our way to an elegant restaurant on the water. A year from that date we were married, much to my mother's dismay. I wore a tea length dress in ivory with seed beads and crystals delicately sewn on. My hair was twisted up in a large, brimmed picture hat.

He was born outside of Lisbon, one of three boys to a wealthy old family whose dad was the Baron of Albufeira, with ties to Salazar. He had a home in Estoril about twenty minutes south of the capital; summers on the Costa del Sol spoiled me. He fathered my daughter, Tagan, but right after she was born, he became ill. Finally diagnosed with stage IV lung cancer, he passed. Neither one of his brothers came to the funeral. They had never met their niece. Uncle Carlos was not Nuno's biological brother—actually a childhood friend who became the only family to recognize my daughter on her dad's side.

We had slowly watched his decline over the years. He was a diabetic, with a heart condition and a habit for thick-cut steaks, strong whiskey, and cigarettes. A couple of years ago, he lost his right leg. He would ride around in an electric wheelchair, which he was sanctioned to, and when we met for dinner, he would let Tagan drive it around the cobblestone streets of Cascais. The last time we visited, he mentioned they may have to amputate his other leg as we all sat in the center of town on a balmy August night sharing laughs and memories.

Apparently, the night he passed, he had driven his electric chair down to Cascais center and ordered a steak on the stone. I'm sure it was a meal he enjoyed. I remembered sitting under one of the umbrellas and placing tender cuts of beef on the flat, hot stone until all the pink was cooked out of it and then dipping the meat in one of the savory sauces that accompanied the dinner. He drank a couple of whiskeys, smoked a few cigarettes, and talked to the waiter about something or other and headed back up the hill to his house. It seemed like a lifetime ago when I first met Carlos. Twenty-five years to be precise. I was so young. Ricardo was correct. It was important to pay our respects.

As Tagan and I walked along the esplanade, the Atlantic pounding on the great boulders beneath our left and the train heading toward Lisbon, or Lisboa, as the natives would call it, on our right. I looked over at my beautiful daughter, who in so many ways reminded me of both my husbands. There were tears in her eyes, and as the sun was setting, it caused them to shine like two emeralds.

"I can't believe we will never see him again."

She didn't usually like to talk about her feelings. "I know, honey—"

She cut me off. "What was Papa like?"

Just that simple question opened a floodgate of emotions in me. Each step that we took reminded me of the first time I visited Portugal, I saw a couple off by the rocks taking pictures, and I was instantly reminded of the day twenty-some odd years earlier when I stood up by the castle on the end of the esplanade by Tamariz feeling like a princess. Nuno stood on the stairs leading down to the sand. As I posed, he snapped pictures on the big black Cannon we had bought until he lost his footing and slipped back onto the granular material. I ran down the steps to help and he snapped at me, embarrassed.

"I'm fine."

I looked stung. He instantly noticed and apologized. We both broke into laughter. That was how we were and at once I missed him with every fiber of my body. I missed not being able to talk to my grandmother. I missed all the things we both had in common that we would chat about, such as books, exercise, tea, good movies. I missed my dad and all the places he was never able to take me and all the lessons he never got to teach me. I missed my grandfather that I called Dede and how uplifting he always was. I missed my Uncle Harry and how cantankerous he could be. I missed seeing Carlos drive his electric chair along the esplanade toward us. I missed them all.

I felt like everything was crumbling down around me. I felt like the loses were too many, and perhaps I had never properly dealt with any of them. It was like grief overload. I was certain Tagan was experiencing similar emotions. Grieving the times, she never got to experience in Portugal with her biological dad. All the places he would have shared with her were not the same shown to her by me. I held out my hand to her. Usually, she would roll her eyes, but she just smiled through the tears she was trying hard to suppress.

The funeral was as nice as a funeral could be. Carlos's wood casket was carefully dropped into the grave site, and the massive stone tomb was pushed back over his final resting place. Along the side of the cemetery, crypts were lined in neat rows just like the one Nuno's aunt's remains were housed in. I missed her too.

Cumulative grief is when current loss brings on feelings of a loss or multiple losses you have experienced in a sequence.

Collective grief is a grief that is experienced by an entire community. For example, the way New York grieved during 9/11.

Inhibited grief is when you display physical maladies such as chronic pain, headaches, or stomachaches instead of grief.

Complicated or exaggerated grief is a grief that worsens as time goes by instead of subsiding. This is profoundly serious and can lead to depression.

Traumatic grief is experienced when a loved one passes unexpectedly. In other words, the grief of a loved one that may have passed away in a car accident.

Chronic or prolonged grief is when you continue mourning for an extended period.

Anticipatory grief is experienced when you are expecting your loved one to pass.

Disenfranchised grief is the grief over a distant relative, a casual friend, a pet, or even an aborted baby.

Distorted grief is a grief that causes you to exhibit feelings of guilt.

Delayed or absent grief is when the symptoms of grief are postponed or not exhibited.

The ten signs of grief I listed above are all ways which people can grieve. Unfortunately, I have personally experienced each one during various losses that I have battled. Some therapists will say the above types are what you experience when your grief is not normal. I respectfully disagree, as there is no normal grief process. It is completely individual to each person.

We arrived safely albeit late. Our plane had a layover in Paris, and we were stuck at the airport for almost four hours. My mother was hosting a party for my stepdad. Ricardo's brother, Mark, was bringing Ric. We were going to meet them both there. We drove from Logan Airport directly to the restaurant. Tagan was on her phone the entire drive.

"Aww, Mama, look at the adorable picture Daddy posted on Facebook. He was so little."

"Let me see honey."

She flashed the screen toward me and showed me a picture of Ric and his older brother with their grandmother. His smile was precious. "What did he say on the post?"

She read: "This is me at three, circa 1961, at my grandmother's farm in Wareham. See my smile? That's how happy I am right this minute to see Sabrina and Tagan."

She paused. "I love Daddy so much."

We arrived just in time to sing "Happy Birthday" to my stepdad. He turned ninety years old. Feeling Ric's arms around me was incredible. I loved him so much.

12

BLOOM

A*nother day at Dana Faber. We were starting to see little signs* of spring on the drive up like forsythia peeking out of window boxes and tulips here and there. We were also able to shed a layer of our heavy outerwear. The days were getting longer too. Not because of the change of season but due to the addition to bloodwork, vitals, doctors' visits, and now Dr. Enzinger added an appointment with a nutritionist as well as the administration of steroids before chemo. They were also slowing down his infusion because he had an allergic reaction his last time; our visits to Boston were getting longer. We started referring to them as dates. On this date, we were able to visit the cafeteria. Ricardo had chicken vegetable soup, and I had tuna salad on a bed of arugula. Slowly my appetite was coming back. Outside, a lovely older woman was distributing prayer cards.

Heavenly Father,

May every cancerous cell be cast out of my body.

May you replace them with healthy ones.

May every spot of this deadly disease

Be wiped out by your powerful hands.

Amen.

I loved that prayer, and I vowed to add it to my daily dialogue with God asking that it be stripped from Ric. Perhaps I should have recited it before meeting with the doctor. A male nurse had weighed Ricardo. His weight was stable. Then we were escorted into one of the many rooms Dr. Enzinger used. They were clean and nondescript with three neutral chairs resting up against one wall. An examining table covered with white paper and a small white desk attached to the wall. Each room looked identical except for the framed prints of different Boston landmarks. It was about ten minutes before he came in.

He seemed particularly cheerful, and I could see a pink collar peering out from under his white coat. He clicked on the computer screen and quietly read for a few minutes. Then he spun his chair around, crossed his legs, and folded his hands on his knees.

"You're still doing good, Mr. Barros. I spoke with Dr. Clancy, and we are thinking about taking those tubes out. I also got the result from your cat scan."

I whispered under my breath, "Please, God, let it be getting smaller."

I could tell Ric was saying the same thing.

"Good news." He smiled bigger.

Yes, here it was. The tumor was shrinking, and it would become operable.

He cleared his throat. "It doesn't show any change at all." A big smile on his face.

I guess that I looked like I was going to burst into tears. Ricardo appeared unphased.

"You know this is just palliative care. Now do you have any questions for me?"

Palliative. I hated that word. I heard it so many times when I was married to Nuno. They would look at me and say you know your husband has a very serious illness. There is no cure. All we can offer is relief from the pain and symptoms associated with his cancer. We want to give you both the best quality of life possible until ... he's gone.

> And the King shall answer and say unto them, Verily I say unto you, Inasmuch as ye have done it unto one of the least of these my brethren, ye have done it unto me.
> —Mathew 25:40 (KJV)

"Doctor, I really want to travel. Would it be bad if I missed one week of chemo? My wife and I have talked about going to Hawaii, and I would also like to take a couple of car trips. I have always wanted to go to Niagara Falls, The Bay of Fundy, and we want to go to New York City as well. What do you think, Doc?"

"Traveling is a splendid idea, missing one week here and there won't make any difference. In fact, next time I see you, try to have the date of your first trip planned, and I will schedule the removal of your tubes right when you get back."

We headed to the infusion as Ricardo ecstatically planned our trips. Niagara, on the Canadian side, was the first place we would visit. Then midsummer he wanted to go to NYC. Labor Day weekend we would head to the Bay of Fundy. I wondered if he had not heard what Dr. Enzinger said about all of this being palliative care.

"Babe, I'm getting better." He had such a spectacular smile.

What is it like to learn you are going to die? We all know death is inevitable. We all live with the potential of death at any moment. Yet we don't give up. So why would we go into a deep state of despair if we were told we were suffering from an incurable disease? At that moment I looked at my husband differently. He had been a successful attorney with so much still to accomplish, and all of that was ripped away from him. This was a huge crisis, and he could have gotten angry or completely given up. He could have even grappled with his faith, become anxious and irritable. Instead, he was living the life that remained. He was so resilient, and I knew part of him was doing it for Tagan and me—all his family. Or was he just in denial?

Ricardo was one of sixteen children. He loved every one of his siblings. Ric's oldest sister was from his dad's first wife— Dorothy Suggs. Carole lived in Philly, and her daughter had become one of my best friends. A couple years older than me, she lived in Huntsville and called me Auntie. When Dorothy left Joe Barros, he married his second wife, Gloria. Gloria gave birth to Jonathan, Brenda, Kenny, Sheila, Stevie, and while pregnant with Ric ended up in the Worcester State mental hospital. He then met a women named Josie and had Scott, Gary, Rene, and Mark. Joe and Josie never married. Instead, he married Marie around the same time he had another son, named Freddie, out of wedlock. Marie and Joe had Rebecca, Ben, and Jacob. In addition, His dad helped take care of Ric's first cousin, Skippy, who he called his brother. I was an only child, and the thought of so many siblings was exciting and scary. I had never met Jacob. In addition to everything else I learned that day, I discovered that that would soon be rectified. Ric's baby brother, Jake, was flying in from California.

Ricardo had not seen him in over twenty years. I knew his trip meant many things—confronting an unresolved family issue, reconciling a lost brotherhood, saying goodbye. Terminal illness causes vulnerability for entire families by unearthing pending emotions that were kept unwrapped for years. The news of our guest made me realize there were underlying issues his siblings and extended family were experiencing. When he was first brought to the hospital, everyone went into crisis mode. Ric was really the glue that kept the family together. The brother that bridged the gap between the older siblings and the younger. His diagnosis disturbed the balance.

After his surgery, everyone came together. The reality of one sibling's mortality pressed problems and grudges to be put on hold. They came together in unity, traveling from across the country to see him. This was paramount for their ability to cope with the imminent loss. It was important for Ricardo to see his family, to feel the love they shared for him, yet it was disturbing as well because it brought to the forefront the very real sense of his mortality, and it disturbed our close family unit in a time when I personally needed that normalcy of our connection.

Six months later, and everyone became ambivalent. He was still a stage IV cancer patient, but he was still among the living, thriving, and getting ready to travel. Everyone was back to their own lives with their own problems. The issues that had been suppressed back in October were starting to reveal themselves. I had not yet witnessed a resolution and wasn't sure at that point if it would happen.

Typically, there are five phases of grief that I have seen families go through:

1. The emergency phase
2. The unity phase
3. The ambivalent phase
4. The resolution phase
5. The remembrance phase

Jacob or Jake, as I began to call him, was approximately sixteen years younger than his brother and not at all what I was expecting. A classically trained musician with a poet's heart and a penchant for red wine and good cheese. We had so much in common. I knew they spent quality time together reminiscing, laughing, crying, and coming to terms with the past. I was so grateful because it was important to Ric besides, I gained a new brother that week. I didn't want to see him leave.

It was a busy spring. One of my favorite nephews had come from Chicago with his mom, which was a wonderful visit as well. I planned our trip to Canada and continued to persist. It was a season filled with life and death, love, hope and disappointment. In addition to all the visitors we received, we also received a letter that crushed Ricardo.

Without question Ric loved his country. He was so proud to be an American and even prouder that he served his country in the United States Marine Corps infantry. It was difficult to convince him to even file a claim, but his sister Brenda and I finally persuaded him. The Veterans Administration needed to take responsibility for his stomach cancer. He drank and bathed in benzene-tainted water for 465 days at Camp LeJeune in Onslow County, North Carolina, from October 1975 to February 1977. This was a lot longer than the thirty days between 1956 and 1986 that President Barrack Obama set. It didn't matter. The neatly typed paper was clear—slightly obese black men were more susceptible to stomach cancer than white men. The Veterans Administration denied his claim. He was heated. I could see the anger and disappointment in his tears.

> Humble yourselves therefore under the mighty hand of God, that he may exalt you in due time:
>
> Casting all your care upon him; for he careth for you.
>
> Be sober, be vigilant; because your adversary the devil, as a roaring lion, walketh about, seeking whom he may devour.
>
> —1 Peter 5:6-8 (KJV)

The loss of a loved one is not the only time we grieve. Grief can be hidden in layers. Sometimes as we grieve our spouse, we feel the loss of financial stability, we can start to regret a poor life choice, a betrayal by a family member from the death of our loved one. My life has taught me that sorrow manifests in many ways. Sometimes we need to let go to grow.

> Keep thy heart with all diligence, for out of it are the issues of life.
>
> —Proverbs 4:23 (KJV)

As the saying goes: Our past does not need to dictate our present. However, It is important to remember that as we grieve, if we can right a wrong, it is okay to do so. If we were in some way wronged, it is okay to peruse resolution. If it was a person, we should welcome his or her willingness to reach out. God wants us to seek out the correction of injustice, He gives us the strength to address the task. Ricardo was wronged by the Veterans Administration, as many who served their country are. While he was battling cancer, he was also grieving the decision. He was also wronged by his primary care doctor who before his diagnosis did not properly care for or diagnose him. It was a difficult decision for me to be left with.

Should I follow course and refile the claim of disability that my husband had originally pressed? Should I seek justice against his medical doctor? These were both difficult decisions that required prayer. In my time of reflection in God's word, I decided to pursue both with the hope that my struggle would affect other widows' experiences. If you are going through a similar conflict, meditate, pray, and even seek out counsel. If your inclination is to pursue a wrong legally, do not feel that you are going against God.

> In those days the house of Judah shall walk with the house of Israel, and they shall come together out of the land of the north to the land that I have given for an inheritance unto your fathers.
>
> —Jeremiah 3:17–18 (KJV)

13
FALLS

As a couple, we had some romantic gateways. Our first vacation on the French side of St. Maarten/St. Martin, lying on the warm sand of Orient Bay. The first time we went to Aruba and despite my fear of the water I went snorkeling in Baby Beach with Ric's encouragement. Cocktails at the Blue Martini in Fort Lauderdale, Florida, salmon fishing in Alaska, sharing my Portugal, and the trip to beat all others—our honeymoon in Hawaii. We had some great family trips as well. There was Disney World when Tagan got to dress up like Belle. Mexico and a rather heart pounding boat ride from Playa del Carmen, the time we trekked through Gettysburg, the Grand Canyon, and all those wonderful ski vacations. Each one was a once in a lifetime experience.

Now we were packed and ready for another adventure. Headed on an eight-hour road trip, I was driving; Ric was in the passenger seat and Tagan was in the back. At fourteen, she still loved stuffed animals, and a soft, plush panda bear sat next to her. I had an entire suitcase of just Ric's medications, along with anything and everything I could possibly need in the trunk. She was busy on her phone, and my husband fell asleep before we drove over the bridge. I was driving west along I-90 heading toward Albany when my mom called me. She was worried. Thought I was foolish to have taken him so far away from home, even though his doctors at BWH gave me the green light. She thought I should turn around and head back home. Her argument was, "What if something happens?"

> Take therefore no thought for morrow: for the morrow shall take thought for the things of itself. Sufficient unto the day is the evil thereof.
>
> —Matthew 6:34 (KJV)

She had a valid point. On numerous nights, I had to rush Ricardo to the emergency room in Boston just like I did Christmas

Eve, and as happy as I was in hibernation those winter months, I was excited to be having a new adventure with my family. Some patients live long past the time the doctor first predicts, like my first husband Nuno, who outlived his two-month expectation by nineteen months. Other patients end up with a complication and lose the fight long before it was estimated to happen. God is the only one who knows. We need to live fully every day.

It was a realization that I came to on that drive somewhere in the great state of New York. Without question, I would continue praying, keeping my open dialogue with God. Expressing my gratitude for every day and still asking for that miracle. But I would make sure that every day that I had with Ric would be treated as a gift. Every day that the three of us got to spend as a family would be like a present wrapped up in a shiny box. It was a lesson I decided I would remember if, for whatever reason, God decided to take Ricardo.

They both woke up in time to appreciate our drive along the Erie Canal. Ricardo knew the history and how it was built to function as a waterway from the Hudson River in Albany all the way to Lake Erie in Buffalo. It was second in length only to China's Grand Canal. He explained the locks to Tagan, and then he hummed the folk song with the same name.

"What's that, Dad?"

"It's a little bit of Americana, honey."

Before long we were all singing:

I've got a mule and her name is Sal,
Fifteen miles on the Erie Canal
She's a good old worker and a good old pal,
Fifteen miles on the Erie Canal
We hauled some barges in our day,
Filled with lumber, coal, and hay
We know every inch of the way
From Albany to Buffalo

Everything was wonderful; our hotel was beautiful with spectacular views of the falls. The next day we had a big breakfast and rode the *Maid of the Mist*. We walked around, drove around, and took amazing pictures. We ventured further into Canada and had an amazing time in wine country— Niagara by the Lake, where our dinner at the Hob Nob was phenomenal, from my trout in a lemon butter sauce with fiddleheads, Ricardo's perfect filet with asparagus, and Tagan's juicy chicken. Then desert, which was a uniquely delicious Ice Wine. The most amazing part of the meal was sitting in a beautiful restaurant, sharing a meal as a family. Such a gift from God. It is interesting how cancer, or any terminal disease, for that matter, makes us see things so differently.

The last couple of days Ricardo needed to rest. He was not using his tubes for food or bile production, but the incision point became infected and was bleeding. After contacting Dana Faber and receiving assurance that it was nothing to stress out over, I felt better. He stayed in the hotel room the last few days, only going out for breakfasts at this spot he really enjoyed. Tagan and I benefited from some mother/daughter time. She started to express some fears she had been suppressing, but I didn't push her to open more than she felt comfortable. Death was very real to her just as it was to me. She had lost her biological dad, and although she didn't remember him, the trauma was real. She also witnessed her great-grandmother die in hospice. She was eight, and it was devastating to her. Shortly afterward, she told Ric and I about her new friend, Althea. Certain she was talking about an imaginary friend who she painted with, we felt safe letting her out. We soon discovered Althea was an eighty-year-old artist who lived two doors down, and they had in fact become friends. Tagan's next heartbreak came when Althea told her she was diagnosed with lung cancer less than two years after losing Nana. She watched Althea suffer until she too succumbed to the brutal disease. Realizing she would never see her Uncle

Carlos again, as she watched her dad, the only dad she knew, battle stomach cancer, Tagan was scared. I wanted to tell her that her father would be fine. That he would watch her graduate from high school and college, walk her down the aisle when she got married, be there to hold his grandchild and all the other things that are so important. I couldn't.

Teenagers, just like adults all react differently to grief. If you are grieving your spouse or loved one and watching your child, teenager, or even adult child grieve a father, uncle, or role model in their life, offering support to them maybe adding to your stress. They need us. The important thing to remember, which I had to learn, is that our children do not necessarily react to grief the same way we may. Allow them the opportunity to do so. They are unique individuals. The most important thing is to: (1) Be there for them. Make time to listen and answer questions that they may have. (2) Be honest and open with them. Don't lie to them and tell them everything will be all right. Be honest about what is going on. Tell them only God knows. (3) Listening to them, their thoughts, and feelings without interjecting your own emotions. (4) Let them know that what they are feeling is normal because there is no right or wrong way to grieve. (5) Check in with their teachers, coaches, religious leaders and make sure they are not bringing harm to themselves in any way. (6) Our children and teens are dependent on us. Some of our worries such as living arrangements, finances, day-to-day activity could be worrying them. Try to encourage them to bring that to God in a daily conversation. (7) Let them know you love them and that will not change.

Those last few days in Canada included quality time being there for my daughter, listening to her, answering her questions honestly, letting her know it was okay for her to handle things in her own way and, most importantly, showering her with love, a little shopping, and the fun house. Niagara Falls was not what

I expected. It was better. Ricardo wanted to drive home, and he did. Stopping only in Herkimer, New York, where I got to find the perfect Herkimer diamond.

Ricardo celebrated his birthday, and the biggest present was knowing Dr. Clancy would remove his tubes. He had told me on the way to Dana Faber that the J tube and the G tube were "the salvation of my life and the bane of my existence." He had not needed them in over thirty days, eating smaller amounts but really anything he craved while we were away. They were going to be easy to take out. The problem was they would not be so easy to put back in if he needed them again.

Successions of good and bad experiences are normal. Sometimes we see Facebook or Instagram pages of friends and family, and everything looks perfect. The bottom side of life is dirty for everyone. Usually when we follow someone's page who is constantly posting upbeat little messages like, "I have everything I need to conquer this day," they are usually posting for themselves. They are feeling some sort of way. They post what they need to hear.

Today was no different—another day of ups and downs. The tumor was measured again, and praise to the almighty, it had shrunk. I made Dr. Enzinger repeat himself twice. I was overjoyed. While walking around on our trip, Ricardo started mentioning a deadening in his feet and fingertips. We had discussed him approaching this to the doctor. Oxaliplatin is a powerful medication. Combined with a couple other cancer-fighting drugs, Oxaliplatin helped to shrink that tumor, and it helped Ricardo to gain the ability to eat again and caused peripheral neuropathy. After carefully quizzing Ricardo, Dr. Enzinger decided it was time to take him off the drug. What was going to happen?

Life by its very essence is complex and noncompliant. I spent years trying to secure a comfort zone. God had a different plan. I think he wanted me to understand that change is inevitable.

I needed to accept the unforeseeable, never-ending revamping of life—to truly be in the now. To relinquish complete control of everything to him. Everything but how I replied to that unavoidable change.

> Remember ye not the former things. neither consider the things of old.
>
> Behold, I will do a new thing; now it will spring forth; shall ye not know it? I will even make a way in the wilderness, and rivers in the desert.
>
> —Isaiah 43:18–19 (KJV)

14

SUMMER

S ummer is such a glorious time. I felt so blessed that I still perceived the season that way. Nuno passed the last day of my favorite month—July. Yet I never associated summer with death, unlike the autumn, which always reminded me of endings. No, summer reminded me of being alive, of joy and hope.

Every morning after my first cup of coffee, I would walk our dog, Gaspar, to the pond, and each magnificent morning I would be greeted by a black capped chickadee who seemed to just sit perched up on a scrub pine not always showing us his adorable oversized and very round head. I told myself that one morning he would not be there singing to me and that would be all right. But he brought me joy. Even Gaspar seemed to look forward to his chirping.

The pond was tranquil, and some days I would sit in one of the rough untreated Adirondack chairs, simply gazing out on the water and soaking in the sun and the quiet. Back home, Ricardo would be up and about all on his own. No tubes peeking through his seersucker pajama top. Depending on the day, I may or may not have ventured to my studio. There were too many pressing things to take care of at home.

The Fourth of July party, family visiting, all of whom I looked forward to seeing, and making more travel plans considering our last adventure had already been successful. One of the next things on Ricardo's list was adopting a new kitten. Check! I had found a breeder in Maine who had a newly born litter of Siberian kittens—a breed that originated in Russia and earned high prices for the claim that they are hypoallergenic. A declaration I believed, as Ricardo was symptom free around our other two Siberian cats. We could visit him Labor Day weekend on the way up to the Bay of Fundy. I couldn't wait to meet the soon to be new addition to our family.

The other pressing matter was a boat. This needed addressing pronto. Cape Cod's boating season isn't that long, and I wanted to make sure Ricardo would enjoy time on the water. We drove up to the North Shore, Gloucester, to look at a used prospect. He didn't think it was worth the money. I didn't really like boats; as a kid I never learned to swim, and the thought of being on the open ocean was a bit frightening to me. The one we ended up purchasing was over on the Vineyard. It was an eighteen-foot Seastrike built in 2007. A wonderful year because it was the year we were married. This boat would be perfect for day cruising and saltwater fishing with a 250-horsepower engine and a center console. Most importantly, it sounded safe. Once again, Ric's younger brother, Mark, came to the rescue, assisting in getting our new acquisition from the island to the mainland. Ricardo was so happy.

> My lips shall greatly rejoice when I sing unto thee; and my soul, which thou hast redeemed.
>
> —Psalm 71:23 (KJV)

Even on the hottest of Cape Cod days, the water temperature is lukewarm. Locals are always debating on which are the best beaches, whether the bay side is warmer than the ocean side and whatever else they can find to argue about. Personally, I believe every Cape beach has an individual beauty all its own, and regardless of which side you are on, the water is too cold except for a few days in August when the ocean is warmer than the air. Those are the days I savor, floating close to the shore until the sun starts to go down. That summer I wanted every day to linger on.

Ric pulled strings and somehow got a mooring off Millway Beach in Barnstable Harbor. We went fishing; we drove it across the water and docked on the shore of Sandy Neck not far from the lighthouse. There were evenings when Tagan was with friends, and Ric and I packed a bottle of wine with some cheese and crackers. We simply sat on the boat waiting for sunset. A few evenings we dined at the Mattakeese Wharf, eating as we looked out on a view that included our little sea vessel.

He was happy and doing well. Ricardo was strong enough to carry the engine down to the dingy, get in the inflatable, and drive it to the Seastrike, which he wanted to call *The Typhoon*, and then drive the boat around to the dock where I would be waiting with life jackets, a cooler, and whatever else we had packed. He was eating. Most importantly, he felt good. I almost forgot he had cancer.

In fact, we were heading to NYC. Tagan and I were driving, and Ricardo alone took the train from Providence to Penn Station, as he had to stay an extra day to wrap up some unfinished business. He arrived looking especially handsome in a suit with his backpack, delighted to regale a funny story that accrued on the trip. In New York, as a family we saw our first Broadway show together, *Fiddler on The Roof.* It was jovial and fun. We walked around, visited our favorite bookstore, The Strand, and left with armfuls of books. We enjoyed eating Indian food, Persian food, and Cuban food. We visited the Natural History Museum and Saint Patrick's Cathedral. Tagan, who was a student at Lee Strasburg School of Theatre and Film auditioned for a part in an off-Broadway play called *Urinetown.* Making her dad even prouder than he already was—she got a part. I realized Ricardo decided what he wanted his daily life to look like. He chose normal or perhaps exceptional. I would have done whatever he wished; looking back, that time was so important for the three of us.

Summer wasn't over; we still had a few more Cape days and then the trip to the Bay of Fundy. He was retreating to his bed a little more than he had been. Dr. Enzinger and the rest of his medical team didn't think anything of it. Summer 2016 had been a summer for the books. When he asked if I would be disappointed if we canceled the trip, of course I said no. I wasn't disappointed. I was concerned.

He had been talking about witnessing the phenomenon of New Brunswick since spring when he had made his bucket list. Numerous conversations were spent explaining that we would need to stay long enough to witness the high tide flowing out for over six hours to a dead low where we would be able to walk along the exposed sea bottom. Then the same day, we would watch 160 tons of seawater flow back in. It sounded awesome and exciting.

"Maybe we should just plan it for next spring, Babe."

Plans are good. "Sure, we can do that."

"What about the kitten?"

He wanted to see the little guy, "I could contact the breeder and ask if she can send us pictures.

"How old is he now?'

I had to pause. "Seven or eight weeks old by now."

It was a summer to remember. A season filled with adventure and love, family, and friends. I was content. I was tired. Most importantly, I was grateful for it all—Niagara, the removal of his tubes, the boat, New York, our life. And now another autumn.

> I will lay me down in peace, and sleep: for thou, Lord, only makest me dwell in safety.
>
> —Psalm 4:8 (KJV)

Photos can be a touchy subject. Some people believe you should not keep photos of the person you loved who passed, and others say it's okay. I disagree with both; unless you are the person grieving, you should not have an opinion. In my home, I proudly display a photo of Ricardo sandwiched between our daughter and I from the trip to Niagara Falls that blessed and beautiful summer. If you want to frame a few pictures, you should. If you don't, then you shouldn't. If you are unsure what would make you feel better, consider a scrapbook that you can take out when you want to look through it and put it away when you feel as though you don't.

15
TEVYA

"For his mercy endureth for ever." This is stated twenty-six times in Psalm 136 in the King James Bible for twenty-six reasons. Why? Because we are not naturally disposed to believe that his love for us is forever. We are not inclined to accept that the pain or suffering that we may have to experience is important to benefit us in any way.

Autumn, the season of my birth. The same season my father died. Yes, he passed October 22, less than a month after my eighth birthday. Autumn, the three months between summer and winter. A somewhat picturesque yet disorganized time that is to me best described as hardy and bleak. Once again it was upon me, and I was worried.

There was a time when I believed that I had seasonal affective disorder. SAD is an actual disease that depletes all your energy, causes depression, and sometimes moodiness. I was certain that was the cause of my mood swings and gloom every fall. I associated September, October, and November with doom and death. I realized what I experienced was more like unresolved grief that would surface as the trees would dismiss their leaves.

Unresolved Grief

If you think you are experiencing any of the following you should consult with a Christian counselor:

1. Severe emptiness
2. Chronic fatigue
3. Digestive issues
4. Self-destructive behavior
5. Preoccupation for your loved one that passed
6. Isolation
7. Feelings of bitterness
8. Feelings of worthlessness
9. Taking on physical symptoms or characteristics of the deceased

10. Depression

Keeping busy helped me to cope when Ricardo suggested allowing Tagan to participate in her play. I didn't refuse. She was ecstatic, and her dad thought it was important that she have something to look forward to. A positive outlet that could benefit her during this especially challenging time. I had to agree, and every Sunday morning I woke around 4:00 a.m. and was behind the wheel by 5:00 a.m. The drive to New York City at that time on Sunday morning wasn't very long—only about three and a half hours. Plenty of time to get breakfast with my daughter and walk her to her practice. The drive was something we both looked forward to. A time when nothing could get between our conversations.

I would spend the afternoon doing things I would not have been able to do. One Sunday, I got my hair done. I went shopping, took an exercise class, or just walked around Union Square. It was "me time" each Sunday. We would be back in the Rover by 6:00 p.m. and home between ten and ten thirty the same evening. A long day that I looked forward to even though it took me away from my husband because it brought me closer to my daughter, something we both needed because I saw what was happening.

When you are a caregiver to a loved one, it is important to also take care of yourself. While you are grieving after loss, it is easy to let your couch call out to you. It's normal to want to stay in your pjs and spend all day watching Netflix. You need "me time," and sometimes binge-watching TV is okay. But also consider calling a friend and asking her to meet you for dinner occasionally. Sign up for a weekly class such as an art class, pottery, exercise, or dance. Something you always wanted to try. Join a book club, a walking group, or the women's ministry at church if you are not already a member. It's easy to withdraw from society and emotionally disengage when we are grieving; these suggestions will help to prevent that from unfolding.

Ric was getting weaker. At night I would have to support him on the way to the bathroom and back to bed. His appetite was decreasing as well. In relation to that, he had lost weight. I brought it up to his medical team, and they dismissed it. He was still getting chemo, but the affects were no longer the same. He wasn't interested in getting out of bed in the morning. But there was something he was looking forward to—our new little furball. Thank God he would ask with excitement every day, "When is that little kitty coming?"

I believed God's love endured forever. I trusted, and still do, that the pain we go through is always with purpose. I also felt that this autumn season would be different; it would be full of life—the arrival of an adorable new kitten, a little marmalade boy that was delivered to us direct from the coast of Maine. The breeder explained that he was a strutter; he certainly did walk right into our life with a little swag and a distinct order of impressing all of us. Even our dog, Gaspar, seemed excited to meet him. All except for the other two cats, who in true feline fashion couldn't be bothered. The Thursday before Columbus Day, Ricardo got all dressed up in a suit for his homecoming. More adorable than I had pictured, with big brown cartoon eyes and a little patch of white under his throat, he had a confident, cocky air about him, and his personage required an appropriate name. When Ric first talked about adopting a new kitten, he suggested Nikki. It was still his name of choice. Tagan wanted the very foreboding Vlad. I suggested the lead from the Broadway play we saw over the summer. The main character and narrator of *Fiddler on the Roof*—Tevya. I won.

I was excited that he arrived for Columbus Day weekend. Ricardo seized the season and all the wonderful things we did together in the fall. Driving to see the foliage, apple picking, fairs. Everything he embraced was done with a spirit filled with fun and adventure. I loved his inner being, his physicality, and his intellect. It was on a return trip from the mountains that he had told me ...

"Life goes on."

Talking about the scientific nature of the season, "You see, Babe, the leaf must fall off the tree to preserve it. To prepare for the coming winter."

When we returned home that Monday night, my favorite cat was missing. Grizzafella was a gray long-haired male that literally walked into my apartment one evening eighteen years earlier. I was married to my first husband, Nuno, at the time. I loved that cat; he would curl up with me on the couch every night and comfort me.

We had a wonderful time leaf peeping in the White Mountains as a family. On the drive back, we had stopped in Topsfield with Tagan. It was the home of the world's oldest fair, and it had the world's largest pumpkin on display every year. Already tired from a few days that included a long hike, a drive along the Kancamagus Highway and just enjoying being together. I didn't care how tired I was; I needed to see Grizzafella. Eventually we found him hiding behind my desk.

My tiny green-eyed boy couldn't even jump up on the couch. I held him, and he seemed to be in pain. When he first snuck into my life, I originally thought he was a girl. A little dirty and very hungry, I named him Grizzabella, after the theater cat who was beautiful but ragged, according to T. S. Elliott. I thought that was an appropriate name. The veterinarian told me my Maine Coon was not a Grizzabella but a Grizzafella. I think he thought he was funny. The name stuck.

The next morning, we brought him, weak and thin, to that same vet. I was informed that Grizzafella was covered with cancerous tumors. Ric said it was best to put him down. His ashes are in a little box under my coffee table. I still think about him; grief isn't just for people. Now I had a new little orange boy to bring us mischief and joy.

I was organizing my travel bag, the one I keep in case I must bring Ric up to the BWH emergency room. A dark olive-green L. L. Bean canvas toiletry bag with a black hook designed ingeniously for hanging on the back of bathroom doors. It was sitting on my bathroom vanity, and Tevya was enjoying a game of batting the hook back and forth with his paws. How adorable, until I looked away grabbing something from under Ricardo's sink. I was startled by a bizarre noise.

"*Awk, awk, awk*—" Tevya was screaming the sound as he swung back and forth with the black metal lodged in his throat.

I screamed, "Oh God, help."

I could not lose this special little guy. He could not perish from my lack of supervision. No, we needed him. He was our new life that Autumn. Ricardo had jumped out of bed. I must have been yelling very loudly because Tagan came flying down the stairs as well. My arm was scratched up badly from his nails as he fought me. But somehow, I removed the hook as my family watched.

We were off to the veterinary clinic. Tevya had esophageal damage, but it wasn't life threatening. His airway was inflamed, so he needed antibiotics, and he had to stay overnight for observation. We were all relieved.

> Trust in the Lord with all thine heart; and lean not unto thine own understanding. In all the ways acknowledge him, and he shall direct thy paths.
>
> —Proverbs 3: 5–6 (KJV)

That night my husband made love to me. It wasn't the first time since his diagnosis; however, it was the last. I am grateful that I didn't realize it. We were able to act as husband and wife for the previous six months. To have that normalcy was important to me, and I felt blessed that he still could. I knew it was important to him too. Not just for the act of having sex but because it was a way of stating his masculinity. When he was first diagnosed, he was in the hospital—, weak and I would say in shock. He was trying to process his diagnosis, and when he came home, the intimacy that we experienced was so different than what we ever experienced before. It was deeper, on a whole different level. I was his caregiver, and I think that challenged his vitality. We had spent nights lying in bed talking about life, reliving moments that were meaningful, mortality. It was a beauty in those nights. But I felt blessed that he had regained strength and still wanted me as his wife.

I think that when a man is approaching the end of life, we assume that he is not thinking about sex. That it's not on the wife's mind either. When you have shared a bed with your partner for many years, when you identify as that person's lover, that doesn't just change because of a diagnosis. It didn't for us. We were always husband and wife until the end.

> Defraud ye not one the other, except it be with consent for a time, that you may give yourself to fasting and prayer: and come together again: otherwise, Satan will tempt you because of your lack of self-control.
>
> —1 Corinthians 7:5 (KJV)

16
GRATITUDE

O give thanks to the LORD, for he is good; for his mercy
endureth forever.

—Psalm 107:1 (KJV)

According to a reenactment at Plymouth Plantation that Tagan went to with family friends, turkey was not served on the first Thanksgiving. The Wampanoags brought deer meat. The Pilgrims brought some sort of wild fowl, which I would think could have been turkey. Who is to say for certain? There are plenty of wild turkey all over the South Shore of Massachusetts. In fact, I have been late for appointments on numerous occasions because an entire rafter of turkeys refused to cross the road, and I could not bring myself to hit them.

For whatever reason, turkey became synonymous with Thanksgiving. Sometimes I think more than giving thanks! Ricardo was no different than anyone else, he loved a good Thanksgiving turkey. So much so that we would drive all the way up to Duxbury to a world class turkey roost called Bongi's. It had been in business for close to eighty years, and our annual stop, which included a turkey sandwich, would also include the wait in a rather lengthy line. No matter, we did every year but the last, so we had to make sure that we would pick out the right turkey.

The dining room table was covered in rich burgundy that was woven with just a hint of gold thread. Our best dishes, the ones Ricardo gave me for Mother's Day the year before he was diagnosed, sat on dark wicker charges that contrasted perfectly with ivory China and the light cloth place mats. Candles flickered at each side of the buttery rich Bongi turkey as it sat in the center surrounded by a stuffing that consisted of carrots, apples, celery, onion, and fresh herbs; there was a green bean casserole, sweet potatoes decorated with little white marshmallows, my special mashed potatoes, tart cranberry sauce, salad, and gleaming moist rolls. It all looked so perfect.

Witnessing Ricardo sitting upright at the head of the table, handsome, cleanly shaven, and dressed in a newly pressed plaid shirt made my number one on my grateful list. I had started to question the actual holiday the year before. If we acknowledge the benefits and favors God grants to us every day, why then should we have a day of Thanksgiving? For the people that do not give thanks daily.

Looking back on my marriage to Ricardo, I am so grateful for those years. I would do it all over again even after knowing the pain I would have to experience. We all want to be happy. However, we don't think that pain is crucial in allowing us to recognize true happiness. You must recognize both ends of the spectrum to appreciate the blissfulness of one. For example, if you are always slightly wobbly on your feet, you do not recognize that you are out of balance—not until you truly feel the difference of being in balance.

Writing Prompt:

On each line, write one event in your life that was painful; next to it write something positive that came from that experience. It may take time, and you may have to search deep inside, but if you do, you will discover that there is purpose in our pain. Watching your loved one die is nothing but anguish, but wouldn't you marry him all over again knowing what would happen?

_____

_____

_____

_____

_____

_____

Unfortunately, pain is unavoidable; happiness isn't the lack of pain but is understanding that pain gives us the strength to accept joy into our lives again.

My mom and stepdad were sitting at the table. Ricardo's younger brother, Mark, came with his daughter, my niece, Hannah. Tagan looked beautiful and took tons of pictures on her phone. It was like she wanted to preserve the day. Who could blame her? I felt so blessed, and when we said grace, I could see the deep gratitude in each person's eyes to be sharing this special meal, to be together. After a rocky start to the autumn, Ric now seemed to be regaining strength, and just two days before Thanksgiving, Dr. Enzinger had told us the tumor shrank again. Praise to the Almighty Healer, we shared the good news with everyone at the table. What a difference from the year before, when the mere scent of food caused him to become physically ill.

Laughter and love were all around. We were indeed blessed and highly favored. I thought he would have eaten a little more than he did, but I wasn't worried because he ate a sampling of everything. Ric assisted in cooking it all. Seeing him in the kitchen was wonderful. A perfect day.

Then his phone rang. My sister-in-law, Brenda, was calling to say "Happy Thanksgiving" to everyone. That wasn't all; there was some bad news too. I could see the change in his facial expression as he listened. I saw one single tear roll down his cheek. He was no longer jovial. Then he hung up and quietly announced that his mother had passed away. Within minutes of telling everyone, he was in the bathroom throwing up. A prime example of happiness and pain.

Sometimes we mourn the relationship we had, and sometimes we can grieve for what could have been. As a widow, we feel the loss of all the experiences we want to share with our spouse. All the special days with family and friends we once celebrated, all the simple moments we once took for granted that will no longer be spent together. We grieve for all the places we wanted to go and know we will never get to go together. These are just a couple of the things that make the loss so hard to heal from.

My husband didn't really know his mother. In fact, his name—Ricardo Miquel—was given to him in Worcester State mental hospital where he was born, by the nurse who had delivered him. I loved his name; it suited him. But his mother had gone mad and could not name him. His dad was in a bad place emotionally. A place of grief although different. She was never released from the hospital, and he never saw her again until he was seventeen and preparing to leave for Camp Lejeune and the Marines. I had only met Gloria twice. Once in the group home where she lived and once at her son's funeral. Ricardo's older brother, Stevie, was paranoid schizophrenic. She was a beautiful woman with radiant dark brown skin and big empty eyes that just stared off into the distance.

He had abandonment issues that prevented him from having healthy relationships with his first wives. Several times in the months leading up to her death, he mentioned wanting to visit her. I think he was scared he wouldn't beat the cancer, and he wanted to try and have some sort of a reconciliation with her. Whenever I would suggest we go, he would find a reason not to. Now he cried over the missed opportunity.

When the house was all back in order, and everyone was gone, I sat in bed keeping Ricardo company and designing our Christmas card. I put a picture from our trip to Niagara Falls, one that we had taken as a family right in front of the falls. I could see the kind older couple that stopped and asked if they wanted us to take a picture. There was one of me and Ricardo on the boat in Barnstable Harbor that Tagan took. My favorite was of Ricardo dressed in his suit holding the new addition to our family—our little orange Siberian, Tevya. A special picture of Tagan looking extremely grown up with her dad standing in front of Penn Station. The Christmas card was a testimony to our year, which despite cancer was a beautiful year. In reflection, we traveled as a family, did somethings we had dreamed of doing for a long time, and spent real, true, quality time together. I knew better than to not take advantage of every day God gave us.

The next morning, after breakfast, he threw up again. He had tears in his eyes. All I could do was hold him. There was nothing to say. He didn't really know his mother, yet he was a part of her. All the things he had dreamed of sharing with her would never be able to be shared. Everything he wanted to tell her wouldn't be able to be heard. So many lost opportunities that only he could relate to. His older siblings had all lived with her. They remembered her. His younger siblings had a different mother all together. I was praying he just needed a little time to work through all the emotions. Then he told me he was in pain.

After throwing up his lunch and his dinner, I called Dana Faber. The office was closed, but there was a doctor on duty. Dr. Pierce was the on-call doctor, and he called me back. His voice was light and young. I explained the situation, and he told me it was normal that he was depressed over the death of his mother. I tried to explain that he didn't know her and that—

"I will write a prescription for an anti-depressant," he cut me off.

He stopped vomiting, but the medication also took his appetite away. I begged him to eat, but he just didn't feel like it. Tuesday, he had an appointment for a small procedure called a transurethral resection of the prostate. It was day surgery. I stayed with him all day except when he was in surgery. I expressed how concerned I was because he seemed to be getting weaker. We were supposed to go to New York City that weekend for my daughter's play. I asked if we should cancel.

The answer I got from the urologist was the same answer I got from his oncologist when he presented for chemo at Dana – Faber the next day. Ricardo had stage IV stomach cancer; his tumor was stable. It was not growing, but he was still a cancer patient. He lost his mother and was vomiting because of the depression over this loss; consequently, he needed the anti-depressants that were prescribed even though they were causing him to lose appetite, which was resulting in weight loss and weakness. I should not change our plans because he wanted to go. Okay, we were heading to New York City.

I was grateful for what they were telling me and still savoring the beautiful Thanksgiving Day that we had the week before. I picked up our Christmas cards, and we both thought they were perfect. Driving home from Boston, Ricardo said he felt like tuna steaks. I stopped at the market and picked up three fresh tuna steaks. When I got Ricardo into the house and comfortable in bed, I set the steaks out and was looking for the large tellicherry peppercorns I had hidden in my spice rack. When I turned around, the steaks were gone. I questioned myself and looked in the fridge. Nope. Then I noticed our kitten, Tevya, and our dog over by the fireplace.

I had to pull the steaks away from them, gently shave off the teeth marks and wash down the fish very carefully. I cooked all three pieces in lemon, pepper, olive oil, black olives, and capers. When my daughter came home, she had a piece and told me it was the best tuna steaks I had ever made. Ricardo didn't touch his but despite knowing what had happened I ate mine sitting in the red wing back chair next to the bed while we watched the news. I told him what the cat had done, he laughed. He just couldn't eat it, but that wasn't why. He took my hand, and we just sat together quietly.

How do you stay grateful when things don't seem to be going right? How do you praise God even when you are frightened? How do you trust him when you feel like you are being let down? Ricardo was failing; I had to push feelings of being crushed away. I knew my world was coming down around me.

But I was grateful for that beautiful Thanksgiving. I didn't want it to be our last. I prayed quietly to myself. I trusted God and believed he had control. I told God I was scared. I also focused on the good things that were happening around me every day as I realized that if the pain wasn't there, would I recognize the joy? I stayed in the moment, in that room, with my hand inside my husband's.

Think about one thing that happened before you read on that was positive, that brought you happiness, and that happened today. I promise there are some. After you write it down, talk with God and tell him you are grateful for what happened and for allowing you to come to the place where you recognize that it made you happy. Let him know that you trust him and that you relinquish control of the situation regardless of where you are in your grieving process. Most important, let God know of your everlasting love for him.

_____

_____

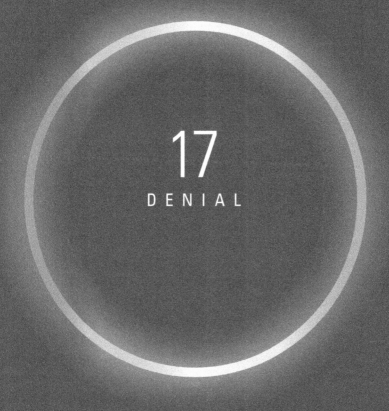

17

DENIAL

> For God so loved the world that he gave his only begotten Son, that whosoever believeth in him should not perish, but have everlasting life.
>
> —John 3:16 (KJV)

"*Let me go.*"

It was what he screamed at me when he lost his balance; perplexed, I told him I would never let him fall. The hotel we were staying in was a lovely, renovated boutique hotel on the Upper West side of Manhattan. It was extremely comfortable with a beautifully elaborate tiled bathroom that could prove to be exceptionally dangerous. I was not letting go till he was safely back in bed. Truth be told, I didn't want to let go at all.

He fell into a deep sleep immediately after. I unpacked and was going over some homework with my daughter when out of nowhere he screamed, "I don't want to die."

"Mommy, why did Daddy just say that." I didn't know how to answer her.

I went over to him and kissed his forehead. I tried to reassure him that he wasn't going anywhere. I mentioned looking into alternative therapy, but he had already drifted back to sleep.

It is not clear whether patients know when they will die or not. Many nurses report that the dying can predict when they will pass. My grandmother talked about seeing a white light from her hospice bed only hours before she left us. My first husband said "*isto e adeus*," when he was admitted into the hospital four days before he died. The translation is, "So this is goodbye."

Perhaps your loved one asked for a dying wish: to see someone special, a visit with a favorite pet, to see a sunset, a particular meal or beverage. You may or may not have been able to fulfill the wish. Talking about death can be devasting. Whatever you did was right. Don't assume you should behave a certain way. We want to create a loving, peaceful environment, one that will help us accept that our loved one is in the final stages of life. Try and respect the dying and their wishes. Most importantly, just show your love.

Tagan asked again. I couldn't bring myself to tell her that sometimes when people are in the final phase of their life, they know, and they are scared. They don't want to leave. Dying is not easy to talk about. Her beautiful hazel eyes had a way of turning emerald when they were filed with tears. Like two big jewels sparkling, she looked at me wanting reassurance that everything was going to be all right. But I couldn't tell her that either. All I could do was put my arms around her, comfort her, and tell her how much I loved her.

The signs were there. It started right after Thanksgiving. He didn't want to leave his bed; he was sleeping for such extended periods, and his appetite had decreased too. Even our conversations were different—shorter, filled with tears. I could see it now. It wasn't that he was depressed about his mother passing; the meds were not why he couldn't eat. His body was beginning to shut down.

The next day I left him for only a brief period. Once to bring Tagan to her play and again a bit later to bring back some food that he wouldn't touch. We lay in bed watching *The Girl on the Train*. I knew he could see the movie because he made various comments with a soft, frail voice as I lay next to him stroking his hair, which was now a light silver. He remembered I had read the book as well.

In the middle of the night, he screamed again, "I'm falling."

I jumped up quickly and ran around to the other side of the bed to find his leg was hanging off the edge of the mattress. "Babe, it's just your leg."

He couldn't lift it up by himself. I assisted him, and although his leg was so thin, it felt like I was carrying a hundred pounds.

He told me he was cold, so I covered him up and tucked the blankets under his feet and lay back down next to him. A few hours later, the sun was already dancing between the small space where the drapes had not quite made contact. The light woke me up.

I showered as I contemplated how I would be able to get him to the theater that night. In retrospect, it is shocking how quickly he declined. Ric walked from the bedroom, through the garage, and into the car. He requested chicken tenders, and so I stopped at the drive-through to accommodate his wish. He ate three of the six breaded pieces. Then he fell asleep.

When we arrived in New York, he couldn't get out of the LR4. It was perhaps a premonition, before we left for the Big Apple, I had requested a prescription for a wheelchair. Ricardo didn't like the idea; I thought it would make it easier for him to move around. If not for that chair, I would not have been able to get him out of the car and up to our room.

Denial is one of the stages of grief. There are therapists that insist that they follow an order, and not accepting the diagnosis is usually considered the first stage of grief. Depression, anger maybe. I even tried to bargain with God when Dr. Clancy first told me there was a massive tumor in my husband's stomach; however, I didn't try to deny it. I had known something was wrong. Those days, the final days, I wanted to deny.

"Would you like a cheese omelet? I could go down to the Europan delicatessen again."

"I can't see."

I grabbed his glasses off the nightstand where I had left them the night before. Tagan was tossing around in her bed as I placed them on him.

"No. I can't see."

I opened the drapes. "Is that better?"

"Everything is black," his voice was weaker than ever before and at the same time agitated. He repeated the word *black*.

I started to think about the leg and now his sight. Thoughts were racing around inside my head. All I could think of was that perhaps he had had a stroke. I called Dana Faber in a panic. Somebody was going to call me back. I didn't wait. I dialed 911 and nervously told them we needed an ambulance. As soon as I ended the call, the phone rang. A man with a thick accent I could not recognize told me his name, which I didn't understand, and after a few questions told me I should bring him to the hospital. It had been the on-call doctor.

As I was hanging up, the EMTS were knocking on our hotel door. Tagan kept repeating "Mommy" and I remember answering questions, I don't know what they were exactly. I also recall watching his long, frail body not at all like the one that once belonged to the man I first met dressed in the handsome blue suit with the shiny gold buttons down the front. Now he was groaning as they carried him roughly through the narrow hotel hallways and into the elevator.

They banged the gurney into the wall, and I snapped, "Hey, watch what you're doing. My husband is in pain."

He apologized. I responded, "Don't let it happen again."

I was not behaving as myself. I don't remember all the details; I assume I rode with him when they transported him to the old Roosevelt Hospital—now part of Mount Sinai. I am not certain, and I don't remember where Tagan was! I knew the hospital well because I was rushed there myself for an eye infection many years ago when I lived in Manhattan. Most of it is just a mirage.

What I will never forget was the doctor—a beautiful young woman with long silky hair and perfectly straight teeth to accentuate her gleaming smile, which she seemed to showcase when she felt nervous. I could tell as she anxiously twisted one hand inside of the other while she spoke words I had never heard before, and she would flash her smile on every exhale. What I did hear was one word several times: leptomeningeal.

I didn't understand what it was. Clearly it had something

to do with his sight. She was telling me my husband was blind. The disease is rare. Only 5 percent of cancer patients have their cancer cells migrate from their stomach to their cerebrospinal fluid. This liquid had circulated to his brain and was contently resting right behind his eye.

"But we watched that movie with the women that rode the train yesterday."

She smiled bigger than before.

"What can you do for this?"

Denial, anger, depression. "Dear God if you just let them fix this, I will do whatever you tell me to."

"I'm not an oncologist." Another big smile.

"He was doing so well; the tumor in his stomach was shrinking. Are you sure he didn't have a stroke?"

"No, Mrs. Barros. I am sorry." She paused; her eyes looked away quickly. "It is a very rapid-moving condition. I don't know that there is any treatment that will help."

"He will never regain his vision." Another smile.

I wanted to scream at her to stop smiling. I did not want to accept that there was nothing they could do. I looked at the pretty young woman right in her deep, dark-brown eyes and pleaded. She told me there would be another doctor coming to speak with me, and they had to admit him.

"I'm never going to read again?"

I stood next to him on the dirty linoleum and held his hand. "We don't know that yet, Babe."

"Hey, watch that damn snake."

What had he just said? What snake was he talking about? His once sparkling brown eyes, now gray, focused on the dingy white wall next to his bed. He shook his head slightly up and down as though he was trying to process everything.

"You know you have to be ready when they come up behind you."

I had tears in my eyes as I brushed the side of his cheek with the top of my hand. "Yes, I will be."

Then, "I love you, Babe."

"I love you too."

I never got to go to my daughter's play that night, but I did see her perform the following evening. I told her how proud Daddy would have been. But I didn't stay for her curtain call. I rushed back to his hospital room. Thank God Ricardo's brother, Mark, had come down from Massachusetts, and my sister-in-law and her family had come in to see my daughter perform and ended up staying with Ricardo for a visit. He loved to have family around. Truthfully, I believe he knew we were there even though he went from being angry talking about historical things like battles and plagues that had happened over a hundred years before to shutting down. When he would get quiet, he seemed aggravated, pensive; he wouldn't eat; he would just stare off. Then he would become very affectionate, my Ricardo.

The doctors in New York were wonderful. They started him on radiation, and I am not completely sure that it made a difference, but at the time I felt as if it did. His mind seemed clearer; I would feed him strained food, and he would eat a little; he always knew I was there. I would only leave his bedside to return to the hotel room for a few hours of sleep, my daughter curled up next to me. She was scared even though she never told me. I was too.

Ricardo expressed his desire to go back home. It was difficult to arrange, but I was able to find a bed at Brigham and Women's hospital and a private ambulance company that would transport him back to Boston. They picked him up around ten o'clock at night. I so desperately wanted to ride with him, but I couldn't because I had to drive our car back, and I had to make sure our daughter was safe. I watched the ambulance drive away with tears in my eyes. All I could think was what if he didn't make the trip. I prayed to God to not let him die in that ambulance.

Around four in the morning my cell phone rang to let me

know Ricardo was admitted to his room. Mark would visit him first thing in the morning while Tagan and I would drive to Boston. Functioning on no sleep seemed normal, and I was determined to make it to his bedside in record time.

Watching someone you love in the final stages of life is a traumatic thing to go through. Sometimes planning on a special way to honor your spouse can be comforting. After Ricardo passed away, I picked several items of his clothing that I felt had meaning or offered me solace. The Vineyard Vines shorts with the embroidered whales, his favorite jeans, the Hawaiian shirt we bought together in Oahu were all included in the amazing quilt I had made from his clothing. When I cuddle up in the quilt, it offers me security and consolation. Here are some ideas to memorialize your loved one that may offer you aid:

1. Have a memorial quilt made from their clothing or make one yourself.
2. Ask family and friends for little notes with special memories and use them to fill a memory jar.
3. Plant a tree, rosebush, or shrub in memory of your loved one.
4. Did they have a favorite saying or scripture? Use it to design a shirt.
5. Use the money you would have spent on a gift every year to donate to your spouse's favorite charity in their name.
6. Make a playlist of all his or her favorite songs.
7. Dedicate a memorial brick or bench.
8. Create a shadowbox with special tokens from your loved one.
9. Start a scholarship fund in your spouse's name.
10. Plant a memorial garden.
11. Adopt a dog or cat and talk to your pet about your loved one.
12. Volunteer or donate to your spouse's favorite charity.

13. Start a blog and use it to speak about your loved one, their interest, or a platform they supported.

14. Run in a marathon that supports a cause that was close to their heart.

15. Participate in a memory walk.

16. Advocate for a cause that relates to your loved one's death.

17. Leave an empty chair at the dining room table for your loved one.

18. Get a special piece of jewelry made from your loved one's jewelry.

19. Plan a family picnic in memory of the one you lost.

20. Write a book.

18

DECISIONS

> Be strong and of good courage, fear not, nor be afraid
> of them: for the Lord thy God he that doth go with thee:
> he will not fail thee, nor forsake thee.
>
> —Deuteronomy 31:6 (KJV)

*D*riving from West Seventy-Fifth Street in Manhattan to 75 Francis Street in Boston was relatively smooth going. My old gray Land Rover made it in a very respectable four and a half hours. But prior to us getting into the vehicle, we experienced delay after delay. Tagan and I had briskly walked down to the hospital to retrieve Ricardo's radiology scans, which were not sent on the ambulance. Once we had them in hand, my daughter was hungry. So, we walked uptown, passing our hotel, to find the Europan Café, which made her favorite cheese omelet. I wasn't hungry, but I knew I needed my strength, so I ordered two. We ate quickly and headed down to the hotel. It was cold, and people in thick black down and fuzzy hats scurried about.

Tagan suggested we purchase some snacks and drinks for the trip. This sensible request was completed at the corner store across the street. We got cheese sticks, water, chewy candies, and chips. In the process of paying for all of this, I must have left the large manila envelope from the hospital because when we got back to our room, I realized I no longer had it. I told Tagan to get everything packed up and ran back across the street. Luckily it was sitting on top of several cases of Dr. Brown's Black Cherry soda apparently exactly where I left it.

I was rushing so much that it was slowing me down. I was anxious and scared. There was no one to verbalize my fears to. If I shared my burden with Tagan, it would have been too much for her. How could I tell my daughter that I didn't want my husband to die? That I knew the end of his life, our marriage, our family, and everything that we knew to be who we were was just about ready to come crashing down around us. I believed that God had a purpose, but I couldn't see it. All I could see was a broken dream. A love torn apart.

As my hands clutched the soft black leather wrapped around the steering wheel, I couldn't help but wonder if he was still with us. As I backed the gray LR4 into the parking spot inside the garage across the street from the main entrance, I thought, please God, let him still be breathing. It was already three thirty by the time we were in the elevator up to his room.

"He doesn't seem to know who I am."

I could see the heartbreak in Mark's eyes. Although they did not share the same mother, Ricardo had close to a foot in height over Mark as well as ten years between them, and Mark's pale complexion was quite different than my husband, Ricardo, with his beautiful chocolate brown skin. Regardless, they were as close as any two brothers ever could be.

"He really is confused." His eyes darted off to the corner of the room.

I don't really remember responding to him or even taking my coat off. I just remember standing over the bed kissing the top of his head. His eyes were staring off into space. My lips gently pressed to his forehead.

"I love you, Babe."

"I will love you forever."

I couldn't believe it; he responded to me. He also knew who I was. I took a deep breath and this time pressed my head up against his. One of the smartest men I have ever met. Now he just lay in the hospital bed with a blank expression on his face with no words coming from his lips. I craved his conversation. The way we could stimulate and challenge each other. How I missed that.

Lost in my thoughts, I didn't even notice the entourage of doctors standing in the doorway. In the middle was a short man with a silk shirt poking out of his white jacket. I didn't notice the name printed on his tag, and when he held out his hand to me and introduced himself, I couldn't understand what he said. Young, handsome with a thick Italian accent. What I could grasp was that this man with the caramel eyes and tan skin that was anxiously spinning a large gold ring around his right ring finger wanted me to make a profoundly serious decision.

My husband frail and confused in the bed next to me didn't understand what we were talking about. Mark and my daughter were nowhere to be found. This was up to me. Should I agree to a surgery on Ricardo's brain that was the only chance he could ever get his vision back, or did I tell him we didn't want the procedure? Without it, they told me days. He would die in days, possibly on Christmas. But putting him through a surgery that could give him a few more months, sight, a miracle. Who knew? Was it worth it?

Our bodies are temples of the holy spirit. We are supposed to take care of them. If I agreed to this surgery, was I interfering with God's will? In Ezekiel, Pharaoh's arm was broken. It was never set properly, so therefore it was never healed. And wasn't Luke a physician?

I looked over at my beautiful husband, his eyes cloudy and gray. "Yes."

"Yes, he needs the surgery," I nervously pulled at the black leather trim that ran down the sleeve of my tunic. I was scared and exhausted, but I believed I did what he would have wanted me to do. Ricardo had told me he wanted to fight. He wanted to live. He never wanted hospice. I sat on the side of the bed with my head comfortably tucked into his shoulder, and I closed my eyes.

> I can do all things through Christ which Strengtheneth me.
>
> —Philippians 4:13 (KJV)

When you are overcome with emotions, your body and your brain are affected. There are no easy ways to restore your ability to function. When we are grieving, even if it is before we have lost our loved one, if we are just grieving the life we once had, we need to take care of ourselves. Perhaps you remember feeling like your world was falling apart, and it probably was. That's how I felt too. Do you remember taking care of a baby? Your mind was numb, and you were overwhelmed. That is called "Baby Brain." I know because I remember going through it with my daughter, and to add to the confusion, I couldn't understand why my husband was acting so strangely. I quickly learned about "Chemo Brain" from my first husband, who couldn't concentrate from all the meds circling through his body. Then I realized I had "Grief Brain." It's real, and it makes everything so difficult to decide upon. If you were left with a life-or-death decision, do not ever regret what you did. It was what God put in your heart.

That night I went home and fell into bed. I got four glorious hours of sleep, and at four in the morning, I took my shower, got dressed, kissed Tagan on the forehead, and drove back up to Boston from the Cape to see Ricardo before the surgery.

Four hours was a lot of sleep for me back then. The insomnia from stress and worry consumed me. It got worst after my husband passed away. Loss is one of the most stressful experiences anyone can go through. It takes a toll out on our physical and mental state. It is, unfortunately, normal to struggle with sleep. A few things that helped me to finally sleep through the night again were simple tools I pray will aid you as well:

1. Go to bed at the same time every night.
2. Wake up at the same time every morning.
3. Exercise every day.
4. Meditate with scripture before bed or when you wake up.
5. Write before bed or when you wake up.
6. Clear your mind before bed by drawing, crocheting, playing music—something that will take you away from what happened during the day.

7. Use comforting scents like lavender.
8. Have a cup of warm tea with honey and/or lemon.
9. Get a weighted blanket.
10. Listen to soothing music.

19

LINCOLN

> If we confess our sins, he is faithful and just and
> will forgive us our sins, and to cleanse us from all
> unrighteousness.
>
> —1 John 1:9 (KJV)

The book I brought sat untouched in my tote bag from The Strand bookstore that Ric and I had purchased during our trip to New York. It was accompanied by my needlepoint and my journal also kept in the bag that was decorated with Gorey cats climbing on overstuffed bookshelves. I did not have the ability to concentrate on any of it. My mind was racing, and my heart was pounding as I walked back and forth on the tiled corridor, heels on my black boots clicking with each step.

Unlike his first surgery, I was waiting alone. It was too close to Christmas, and everyone had other family to be with. I felt somewhat isolated. Of course, Tagan would have been there waiting with me if I asked her to. I wanted her to sleep and then scheduled family friends to pick her up. My mind took me to a Christmas long ago when I was sound asleep in my bed and startled from the ringing of our phone. I remembered hearing my mother get up, the bed squeaking. I could still hear the sound that princess phone that sat on her dresser made when she picked it up. My grandfather died that night. There were two big gold chairs in our living room, one on each side of our Christmas tree. My grandmother sat in one and my mom in the other. I was curled up on the couch crying. The lights from the tree looked blurry through my tears, and for several years Christmas was never the same. My mom would have come if I asked her.

I started playing the whole thing back in my head. How first he could not sleep, and my crazy premonition—the number ten. How he started losing weight, throwing up, and being told it was nothing. When he was brought to Boston for a so-called ulcer. Finding out it was really stage IV stomach cancer. Those damn tubes, Niagara Falls, all the love and prayers. Our little Tevya scampering around the house. Ricardo's mother, Gloria, passing away. Tagan's play and the accomplishments she achieved during so much turmoil. New York City. Being told my husband was blind only a night after watching a movie together. It all brought me there to that sterile waiting room in Brigham's, praying as I stood there with my bag, my coat, my tote, too exhausted to sit down and too nervous to stop pacing.

"Mrs. Barros." I recognized the accent.

I spun around. "Yes, Doctor."

"Your husband is resting quite nicely; you can see him shortly. We will have him brought up to his room when he starts to come to; why don't you get something to eat, and then you can meet him there."

Thank God he was okay. I didn't want to eat. I wanted to rest. To close my eyes. I sat down on a big leather reclining chair and took a great big breath as I drifted off to sleep.

The doorbell rang, but by the time I had run from the kitchen to get it, the UPS driver had already left the heavy, slightly damp brown box on my front step. I immediately knew what it was, so I carefully carried it inside. I was excited. Christmas was always a favorite time for me, and I spent a lot of effort decorating for the season, cooking, and planning out the perfect gifts for each person on my list. When I saw the bust online, I knew I had to order it. One of the very first things I remember him ever telling me was how much he always wanted a bust of Lincoln.

"Hey, Babe, who is it?" The doorbell had awakened him.

"Oh, it's just a package," I responded slightly winded as I pulled it into the living room.

"What is it?"

"Your Christmas present."

"Can I have it now?"

I went into the bedroom laughing as I explained to him how excited I was to give him this present and it was just too special to let him have before Christmas morning. I wanted to wrap it up in shiny paper with the big gold bow and present it on Christmas Day. I wanted everything to be just like it was before he was diagnosed with cancer. I wanted the best Christmas ever. I didn't tell him all of that; I just kissed him and carried the heavy box downstairs. Our basement was partly finished; it also had a big closet, an exceptionally large storage area, and a room that was once a coal bin. We turned it into what Mark affectionately named "Santa's Workshop." I placed Lincoln, who was so much heavier than I had imagined, on the folding table and looked for a large roll of festive paper.

"Hey, hey."

I yawned a startled yawn. My eyes wide open looking around. I wasn't in my basement. I was still in BWH.

"Mrs. Barros, your husband is upstairs. He was looking for you."

"Oh. Thank you."

I had fallen asleep for over three hours—my purse, book bag and coat a lumpy weighted blanket. My body felt stiff, but I had needed that sleep. I was still slightly confused trying to figure out where Lincoln was and why I hadn't just given it to him that Thursday before we left for New Yok City, when it first arrived. I stood up. I knew BWH better than I had ever wanted, so I made my way to the towers of 75 Francis Street. The curved clover leaf building had pods labeled A, B, C, and D. Ric had been on 12C, 6A, 7B, 5B, and lastly, 4C. I took the elevator up to the fourth floor. His room was empty. He had been on so many floors, yet I knew that had been his room.

They moved him to the D tower. When I found him, I couldn't believe how he looked. All his hair was shaved off the left side of his head and replaced with a giant scar that ran from his forehead alongside his skull. He had a large blister and several smaller ones on his upper lip. He was making a chewing motion with his jaw and rocking his head from side to side.

I put my stuff down on a chair and sat on the side of the bed.

"Hey, Babe, I am so happy to see you."

I put my head on his chest, and I felt his arms around me.

"Hey, Babe, I missed you."

"I missed you too. I was waiting for you to get out of surgery."

"I had surgery?"

"Yes, Babe, and you're doing great."

"I love you."

"I love you too, forever," I could feel him hug me tighter, and it felt so good.

"Now, listen, this is important. Life has too much confluence. People have a hard time picking. So, then when it's time to actually do it, they worry." He cleared his throat.

I stroked his arm. "Yes, Babe."

"So, there you have it. Those are the kinds of people I'm talking about." He licked his lips, and I noticed another large white sore on his bottom lip. His eyes were closed, "Because if you do something good every day, if you try, no one should get hurt by your life." He rocked his head back and forth on the pillow.

I wondered what he was thinking about. Did he feel like he had hurt someone? Was there something he regretted doing or not doing? Was it his past wives, broken relationships? I knew I was the fourth Mrs. Barros. His first wife was a lovely Japanese woman he fell in love with as a young marine stationed in Okinawa. They were married. Shortly after, he was sent somewhere. I don't remember. When he returned, she had passed away from damage to her liver. She had a son from a previous marriage, and I knew he regretted not looking for that boy. When he returned to the States, he met a wealthy want-to-be artist who broke his heart. He got married to the second Mrs. Barros on the rebound. She thought she was the first; she also thought she was the only one. He was not a faithful husband at the time. Eventually they got divorced, and he re-married the third Mrs. Barros, who believed she was the second. Four years later, that marriage began to crumble. Was all this haunting him?

"Someone has to feed the bill you paid." He corrected himself, "You made."

I stayed with him till almost midnight. He had been sleeping for over ninety minutes when the nurse came in to tell me I should go home. I had to talk to my mom on the car ride home so that I would not fall asleep. It was a long drive. Exhausted, depleted, lacking nutrition, I was desperate for a shower and my bed.

When people are dying, they will show remorse. Not for the material things they didn't get. Not for how much is in the bank account. For not having had the courage to live the life God had planned for them. For not spending quality time with their loved ones. For not telling someone how they truly feel. For not maintaining special bonds. For not allowing themselves true happiness. I am not sure what my husband was talking about, but I knew there had to be a regret. Learn from your loved one that passed. Don't feel as though you must stop living as well. Continue the path God planned out for you.

On Christmas Eve, I was asked to join a meeting. Father John, a priest that my husband loved and was really comforted by sat on one chair across from the door. He had kind eyes and a sympathetic smile. Dr. Clancy was at the table; Dr. Enzinger was not present. Two other women I had never seen before also attended. One was a social worker with curly silver hair and high cheekbones; the other women introduced herself, but I couldn't remember who she was or why she was there.

When my nana passed, it was in a hospice house. For some

who wish hospice, it is wonderful. Nana was ninety-seven, and she lived with my mom since my grandfather passed. I understand that sometimes responsibility is exhausting. On the previous Sunday, I had taken Nana to a show with Ricardo and Tagan. Yes, she needed assistance, but she was almost an entire century old. I also got her Chinese food. Monday, I brought her a romance novel. Tuesday when I stopped by, she had read the entire book and wanted to tell me all about it. Wednesday when I called, my mom told me she had to bring her to the hospital because she was having stomach pain. Thursday, I called Cape Cod hospital to check on her. She wasn't there. I called my mother back and after careful investigation found out she was at a hospice house. I was shocked. She did not have terminal illness; she was just old. I immediately went to see her. She was sitting up and asked if I had any perfume. I gave her my channel rollerball.

"My stomachache is all better; I want to go home now." She looked great.

I asked at the desk, and they told me I could not remove her. I was not her power of attorney, nor did I have any right to do so. The next day I came to see her, and she was on morphine. I asked her if she had felt pain. She was adamant that she wanted to return home. The next morning my mother called us. She had gone into a coma. She died that same day.

Ricardo was appalled at what happened, and I went several weeks without talking to my mother because of it. He made me promise I would never put him in a hospice house, and I would always stay true to my words, not just because I would want someone to do that to me but because it is the right thing to do.

> My covenant will I not break, nor alter the thing that is gone out of my lips.
>
> —Psalm 89:34 (KJV)

"I am sorry; I will not allow my husband to be put in a hospice house."

Father John tried to tell me how hospice was originally started by nuns. Dr. Clancy explained to me how every avenue of care was exhausted, the social worker told me I didn't have an alternative. I was weary, but I was not weak. I stood up a determined wife as in love with her husband that day as the day we walked down the aisle. I had promised.

"No, I am sorry; I want my husband home with me."

The heavy-set woman wearing the white coat over her black slacks moved forward in her chair. She placed her elbows on the wood conference table and looked me straight in the eyes. Then she calmly proceeded to explain to me that if my husband lived through Christmas, they would arrange an ambulance to bring him back home to Cape Cod. I would be cut off all services. There would be no medicine, no nurses coming to help clean him up, no hospital bed or supplies of any kind. No support teams. I watched her eyebrow rise and lower as she spoke. I saw the slight smirk on her face. I asked God to help me erase all feeling of animosity I had toward her.

I took a deep breath and stood up. "Understood. That is a lot better than watching my husband die in a hospice home when he specifically explained to me that would not be what he wanted. He wants to be home surrounded by his family."

I tugged the red plaid jacket I was wearing. "Thank you all for your time and consideration." I forced a smile.

When I left him that Christmas Eve, I was so scared I would not see him again. I wanted to curl up in the hospital bed and fall asleep next to him. Everything was so different from the previous year with the magic of the carolers and our wonderful party. I ran my fingers over the cross he had given me that night one year ago. It had been an incredible twelve months. I wanted to scream "Why?" but I knew the only constant in our lives is God. And, of course, as cliché as it sounds—change.

Christmas morning was nothing like past years. Tagan and I woke up early; we exchanged presents alone on the couch because I wanted so much for her to have some normalcy. I was so glad I had come home. She needed me too. We hadn't been to church; there weren't any family gatherings. Just the two of us in the big cape house rushing through a quick breakfast after the gifts were open. Just me struggling to get Lincoln's head into the back of the car.

There was hardly any traffic the entire trip up to Boston. Tagan and I played the Toby Mac Christmas CD, but it just didn't feel like Christmas Day. I knew she felt scared. I knew she was worried and sad, but she didn't want to talk about it. In retrospect I realize I didn't want to talk either. I had too many thoughts running through my head that I couldn't make sense of. I was simply happy to have her sitting next to me. I reached for her hand, and she put it into mine.

Ricardo was still alive, lying in his hospital bed waiting for us. I brought Lincoln up to his room, and he was able to move his hand over the smooth plaster surface feeling the eyes, nose, and lips. He smiled a great big Ric smile. Then he told me he felt successful because he finally had a bust of Lincoln to put in his library. A few minutes later, he told me he didn't want to go to AA.

"Babe, what are you talking about, you don't need AA!" He looked confused.

He was a social drinker at best. Then he wiped his nose and said, "stop bugging me."

I replied with, "I love you, Babe."

"I love you too."

If only I had given him the dang head that day the package had been delivered to the door. Why didn't I carry it into the bedroom and open it up right there by his bed? I could have taken it out of the moist cardboard box and carefully unwrapped it from the bubble wrap right in front of him. Lincoln could have kept him company the whole week before we left for New York. He would have seen the beautiful alabaster head next to him, and he would have known that it was his Christmas present.

The wouldas, shouldas, couldas, were trying to attack me. Yes, had I given Ricardo the beautiful bust of his favorite president, Abraham Lincoln, that cold drizzly morning it arrived, he would have gotten to see it with his own eyes. But that wouldn't have changed his stage IV cancer diagnosis. That wouldn't have changed the fact that the cancer spread into his brain and took his sight. Nothing I could do would change any of that. I was powerless. God was in control.

God is the one in control for all of us. Nothing we do can cause the outcome of loss to be changed. It is God's will. When we accept this, we also accept that we have no power and sometimes when we are grieving that is a difficult thing to do. Take a moment and a separate sheet of paper and write down whatever guilt you are still holding onto.

Know that the outcome would have been the same if your actions were different. I know everything that I felt guilty about in relationship to my husband's illness because I took the time to write them down, and there is a power in writing it down. In understanding those things. I had to really think about each one, not just Lincoln's bust, and I realized that if I had acted differently, nothing would have changed. Ricardo still would have been diagnosed with stage IV stomach cancer; it still would have spread to his brain, and, yes, he still would have gone blind. Accepting this truth and God's love helped heal my heart. I pray you see that too.

Take the paper you wrote on and cut the paper into little pieces; on a walk, let it go out into the universe. It is not your guilt anymore. If you prefer, light a candle, and say a special prayer asking God to help you release the guilt, and burn the paper. Allow all your negative thoughts to go away.

And hereby we know that we are of the truth and shall assure our hearts before him.

For if our heart condemn us, God is greater than our heart, and knoweth all things.

—1 John 3:19–20 (KJV)

20

ENDINGS

> A time to be born and a time to die; A time to plant, and
> a time to pluck up that which is planted.
>
> —Ecclesiastes 3:2 (KJV)

There is a picture of our hands, the three of us. Just our hands. One of the nurses took it on Christmas Day. Ricardo's brown skin over Tagan's young, pale hand and my callused one grabbing on with all my strength. Our last Christmas together spent in the cold, sterile hospital room, no home-cooked meal, no family or warm fireplace with stockings neatly hung. Just the three of us and Lincoln. I am so grateful that we had that, though. The next day I was told I could change my mind. Ricardo could be transferred to a hospice house near the Cape, or he would be released and brought back home. I tried to explain to them that it wasn't for me to decide; my husband had already done that. So, they were discontinuing all treatments including food and medication. Every avenue had been exhausted, and they wanted to reiterate that, just in case I was confused. There was nothing they could do anymore, and I could see it.

Gurgling sounds were emanating from his chest; he was even more confused speaking to family that had passed away year's prior. Falling in and out of sleep, then wide-awake regaling a Bible passage with completely clear mind. I felt so painfully helpless as I watched him, holding his hand, stroking his hair, telling him I would love him forever. I was already mourning all the things I knew would never happen. The trip to Hawaii on our tenth anniversary now only a few weeks away, the Bay of Fundy, Ricardo standing next to me as we watched Tagan receive her diploma for high school and college; these things would never happen. And what if I couldn't take care of him like I promised, what if I did something wrong? Floods of thoughts floated through my head. How would I ever make sure his funeral was just as he would want it to be? I would have to be strong for our daughter and for the promises. It was obvious there were no more miracles to pray for. My husband was dying, and so I prayed for strength.

He was brought home in an ambulance, and the paramedics laid his body—once well over two hundred pounds, now eighty—in our bed. There would be no visiting nurses to help roll him over, so I placed an extra bed sheet under him. I had to use my own strength to pull him up, and the sheet made it easier. I remembered the trick from taking care of my Uncle Harry. It wasn't easy but I was thrilled to have him in the house with me, lying next to me.

Hospice is different in every state. I have a family member that has been in hospice for over two years in Alabama. She is cared for with dignity, brought food, a nurse to check her vitals, and shown love as well as support. When a patient decides hospice or palliative care is the right choice, the service can be a comfort and a blessing, especially in some places. Sometimes patients can be admitted to hospice homes, or hospice nurses can be sent to the terminal patient's home, and the service is a huge support for the dying and the family as well. Not everybody wants the service, and it shouldn't be the only option for a dying person. My nana didn't want to be in that hospice house; she wanted to be home, and without the morphine she would have died on God's time. Instead, the process was sped up. My heart was broken knowing that my sweet grandmother who cared for so many people including me died that way. They say hospice is dying with dignity. I have only seen hospice as euthanasia. My nana had it forced upon her; she didn't pick, and both Ricardo and I resented that. I forgave the situation because it is what Jesus taught us to do. Just as it states in Matthew 6:12 (KJV), "Forgive us our debts, as we forgive our debtors."

Ricardo was appalled with what happened. That night when we curled up next to each other in our bed he told me, "I never want to be put in a hospice house like that, and I don't even want a hospice nurse around me."

"Me either, Babe."

When he was first diagnosed, he reminded me of the conversation. I assured him that I would never go back on my word. Sitting alone with my dying husband, using a small pink sponge attached to a thin white stick, I dipped into water and then placed that on his tongue to keep him hydrated. I thought how unfair that they would not allow him some intravenous without morphine. Each day was spent cleaning him, washing clothes and sheets, holding his frail body, and telling him everything would be all right even though I knew it could never be all right again. Without question, one of the most difficult things I ever had to do.

Painfully I watched him grunt and cry out, his breath heavy and labored—the sound of death emanating from his chest. Tagan would come into the room for short periods of time. It was taxing for her to see, yet she would lay next to him and tell him how much she loved him. I wanted her to be there with us every minute, but I knew it was too much. I needed to savor every second with him that I could. We all deal with death differently.

On Saturday, New Year's Eve, we told him 2017 was coming in. I am not sure he really understood. He didn't speak. The television was on when the ball came down in Times Square. I had a glass of wine and was reminded of all the previous years— the joy the promise of each new year would bring. By January 1, I was relieved that he made it into 2017, and I was exhausted; I could hardly keep my head up. As tired as I was, I did not want it to be over, yet I knew that at any moment he could take his last breath. What a blessing that he wasn't taken from us as we rang in the New Year; I prayed he didn't die January first either. Ironically, I learned that my girlfriend's husband passed unexpectedly. I had been so wrapped up in caring for Ricardo that I didn't even know he had taken ill. How strange life is. What a clear reminder that we never know what one day will bring to the next.

As a couple, we had been right by each other's side since the day we met. I could just be myself with Ricardo—sexy, elegant, or a hot mess, he didn't care. I always felt wanted, loved, and special. I could sound like Einstein or spit out utterly ridiculous bits of useless information; he would still listen, laugh, and respect my opinion. We had mutual esteem for one another; we understood each other; we got each other. Our love was unconditional. We were meant to be together. Thinking about him not being next to me, not being there to share my day, my life—well, it was excruciatingly painful. Yes, I wanted to be with him every single minute he had left. I wanted to be with him when he took his last breath. Apparently, he wanted me there too.

Tuesday my brother-in-law, Mark, came over. He told me I needed to get out of the house for a bit. I went to my studio. My mind wondered if he would leave when I was not there. Was that what he was waiting for? No phone call, no text, so I headed back home. Friends had stopped by. I found them helping to get him cleaned and changed. Canja, a delicious Cape Verdean version of chicken soup, sat on the counter waiting for me. I didn't want any. I was more exhausted than if I had stayed home doing everything for him. I lay in bed; he kissed my head and put his arm around me. Our friends left, Tagan went upstairs to bed, and my brother-in-law, Mark, headed up to the guest room. The TV was on, I think CNN, I can't be sure.

In a soft faint voice, he whispered, "I love you."

It was the first thing that he said in a couple of days.

I answered, "I love you forever."

I was so tired; I rested my head on his chest. I could hear him breathing heavier, sporadic, and then nothing. The rattling sound had stopped; there was no more labored movement of the chest. I screamed so loud; I could not stop yelling, and then inarticulate high-pitched mournful wailing started. I could hear myself, but I couldn't control it. The EMTs came, and because we had declined hospice care, were forced to try to revive him. I clearly remember them ripping open the new, clean, flannel pajama top in black watch plaid and pounding on his chest; our dog was going crazy, and I was still screaming and crying.

I believe my brother-in-law drove us to the hospital, Tagan and me. The three of us sitting around my beautiful husband's cold, lifeless body. Tagan looked so broken. Her pale skin looked clammy, and her pupils were so big that I thought her eyes were going to pop or that she was going to throw up. It made me realize she didn't really believe her dad would die until that night. She was holding out hope, praying for the miracle.

I felt like such a horrible mother because I couldn't comfort her. I just sat there; the sobs were gone. They later told me I had gone into shock. She was the one holding me, wrapping her arms around me, and kissing the top of my head. Mark was on the phone calling family. I could hear him repeating what people were saying. It wasn't registering.

Fifteen years before, my feelings were similar, sitting in the same hospital on Cape Cod waiting for my first husband, Nuno, to be pronounced dead. To make his death official. I left right after. Went back to my mother's house and picked up my daughter; she was so tiny. I remembered how I whispered in her ear, "It's just you and me now." It wasn't. Ricardo came to our rescue like a knight in shining armor gallantly sweeping us up and carrying us off to his castle. This time was different; this crush was heart-wrenching. I felt like an egg that had been dropped on the tile floor in the kitchen, broken with my yolk oozing out all over the place. There was no way to salvage a broken egg.

A doctor came, a priest, and then the doctor came back. They told us we could stay for as long as we wanted with the body. We sat there, the three of us, till five o'clock in the morning. I would have stayed longer. It was time to leave. When I kissed his forehead, it was ice cold on my lips.

When I got home, I crawled into bed under the blanket that was covering Ricardo when he passed. I curled up wondering if he had heard me screaming, wailing like I did? They say that after a person stops breathing, he or she can still hear what is going on around them. I worried I had disappointed him. I didn't pray to God because I didn't feel like I had anything to say to him. I couldn't say thank you. I was not grateful that dreary January 4 day. There was nothing, no one I wanted to pray for. I felt so abandoned, alone, and helpless.

Reliving that night, the morning after—it's still painful. It always will be. But I needed to do it to come to terms with a few things: (1) I had to realize all the blessings God had bestowed on me. The mere fact that I had the opportunity to be married to such a wonderful man. That I was given the ability and strength to be there for him, to take care of him at the end. (2) My husband would have been proud of me regardless of how I handled his passing. There is no preparation for that moment. No guidebook on how to conduct yourself. I did the best I could do. (3) I was not alone. I had my beautiful daughter, family, friends, and my most important relationship, the one I had with God. I want everyone that reads this to know that the relationship you have with God can heal you in a way you can't always imagine. His love for us is what we need when we are lost, broken, crushed.

At this time, you want to retreat, but there are so many responsibilities. You must contact the funeral home, notify family, perhaps call an attorney, order flowers, write an obituary, and collect numerous documents. Then you must deal with banks, financial advisers, the insurance company, perhaps Social Security, the DMV, and credit card companies. The list goes on and on. But the most important thing you need to do is *be careful = full of care for yourself.*

Remember:

1. Don't try to ignore your pain. It won't make it go away.
2. You don't have to be *strong*. It's okay to let people see you cry.
3. Crying is not the only reaction to grief. It's all right to show your pain in other ways.
4. There is no time frame to grief.
5. There is no right or wrong way to grieve.

21

WATCHING

T*hose days leading up to the wake and funeral were foggy.* Almost like some sort of abstract picture, I couldn't quite tell what was going on. I do remember sitting at Ricardo's beautiful antiques desk writing his obituary on his big Dell desktop. Twisting from right to left in the oversized, scuffed up, burgundy leather chair he had once sat in while voices recalling happy days flooded in from the kitchen. I know I flipped through numerous poems before choosing one for the program I designed. It was W. H. Auden's "Funeral Blues" that somehow seemed most appropriate.

Bring out the coffin; let the mourners come.

I also remembered it from the movie *Four Weddings and a Funeral.* I knew it was also referred to as "Stop All the Clocks," and was one of the most beloved poems in all Great Britain. Ric loved that I enjoyed poetry and purchased a book of Auden's for me. It was a perfect choice because:

> He was my North, my South, my East and West,
> My working week and my Sunday rest,
> My noon, my midnight, my talk, my song;
> I thought that love would last forever: I was
> wrong.

I can see myself standing up on the creaky wood floor in my black sweater dress choosing flowers at the same florist shop that did my wedding bouquet and thinking the whole time "for nothing now can ever come to any good." I know I was insistent on one of the more expensive caskets because I couldn't think about budgets or debt. I distinctly remember Mark took me to the mall so I could pick out a black dress for the wake. It was a simple classic dress with a scoop neck and lace sleeves that I knew I would never wear again. Afterward, he took me to dinner at Hearth and Kettle. The rest is unclear. Those days' events are not crisp in my mind; they are more like a mirage.

I never felt the winter in my bones; it was as though my body was numb. I can't recall specific details, people, scents, or sounds. The pictures of those days are blurry. The wake itself is somewhat clearer. I will always remember standing in my new black pumps with the burgundy suede toes that hurt so bad. How red and swollen my feet were when I was home tucking them into my comfy old house slippers. The faint scent of lilies, and endless hands to shake. Tagan standing on my left strong and beautiful in a somber dress that made her thin, strong body look almost frail. She wasn't; at fifteen, she had already lost two fathers.

Then it was over; everybody went home. The house, once cozy and secure, just seemed big, empty, and cold. There was so much to do, I had stacks of unopened mail, piles of bills that needed to get paid, tons of trash that needed to get taken to the dump. On top of all that, there was legal stuff to take care of, lawyers that needed to be contacted, old clients of Ricardo's that were leaving messages and needed return phone calls. His old office that needed to be packed up and still people that needed to be notified. But I could not concentrate on any of it. I was so run down from the lack of sleep, my inability to eat, and the stress. It all just piled up into one big mountain that was too big for me to climb.

I would wake up and put on Ric's warm plaid flannel shirt, the one from the Pendleton catalog that he had wanted for Christmas two years ago that still smelled like him. I would wear it with a pair of leggings and sit with my cup of coffee, hands wrapped around his favorite Marine Corps mug for hours just thinking what I would do when his scent wore off the shirt. Before long, I was drinking six cups of strong black coffee each morning while just sitting staring out at the cold Cape Cod winter.

One morning a huge oozing cold sore appeared. It covered the entire left side of my lip. It felt foreign and uncomfortable, yet it was in a strange way a pleasant distraction. Until it crusted over and somehow manifested into a stuffy nose, which triggered sneezing and a sore throat. All of which turned into a bad case of bronchitis. Before long I discovered a rash, which ended up being diagnosed as shingles. I was a physical and emotional mess. Eventually I was diagnosed with pneumonia, which was hard to shake because I also had insomnia. I couldn't sleep in our lonely king size bed, and my daughter couldn't sleep in her room. One night while watching TV with me, she fell asleep on the black leather recliner; shortly after, I must have fallen asleep on the couch. We got a combined eight hours that night. It felt blissful, and so that is where we ended up every night.

Perhaps this is where you are right now. When you hear someone say heartache, it is true. Our hearts can literally ache. Yes, grief affects us both emotionally and physically. Grief can cause fatigue, loss of appetite, nausea, pain in the stomach as well as the chest, difficulty breathing, insomnia, and headaches. Now is the time for self-care. Try to plan short activities that will give you some enjoyment. Perhaps nature walks, join an exercise class like Pilates or even adult dance, try to investigate healthier eating habits, schedule a massage, or go away for a while. That's right, there are emotional symptoms associated with grief, and there are physical symptoms that manifest as well.

I started praying, "Dear God, please let me be able to sleep soundly through the night." I knew sleep plays a vital role in our mental and physical well-being. If we do not get quality sleep, we do not have a good quality of life. Desperate for some restful nights, for true relaxation, I rented an apartment in New York City for six weeks that first summer. It was just a little studio in Yorkville, on the Upper East Side of Manhattan. I guess that is how God answered my prayer because we needed to get away. I spent a lot of money on things like the theater, sushi, and new clothes we did not need just to try and heal my brokenness. Manhattan helped me to accept that Ricardo was gone, to build an even closer bond with my daughter, to begin processing my emotions, to start exercising again, and practicing the self-care I knew I needed.

When we returned to Cape Cod in September, Ricardo had already been gone for nine months. We were both sleeping a bit more; I was able to concentrate and quiet my mind enough to read a little again, to do chores around the house, and to go back to work. I had redeveloped my daily exercise routine to include basic spinal movements, breathing, stretching — things that I had done all my life and taught for most my entire adult life. I was getting healthier, stronger, calmer. Ironically it seemed like people were resentful. Some friends and certain people that worked for me didn't feel like I deserved those things. I heard rumors— "I wasn't grieving properly," "it seemed like I didn't miss my husband, and I had moved on with my life," or "I seemed depressed and missed him too much; I should be able to let go."

There is no right way to grieve. Nothing in life can prepare a person for the death of a spouse, a child, a relative, even a close friend. Even when we watch someone suffer, when we take care of them day after day, death catches us off guard. Nothing is more stunningly final then watching someone take his or her last breath. I have had to watch it three times. Some folks are blessed enough to go their whole life without ever watching someone die. I wish no one would ever have to experience loss or grief, no one would have to see it with their own eyes, or have to hear it, because death isn't silent, and that no one would ever feel the coldness of death because it is frigid.

When my dad died, I was only eight, and I will always remember that October day. I had made him a card in school, and I couldn't wait to bring it to him. My mom picked me up, and we headed toward home. I asked why we weren't going to the hospital. She smiled at me. When we got home, my nana was chopping an onion by the cold, white, porcelain sink. Her eyes were red but not from the onion. I didn't know that at the time.

My mom sat me up on her knee and said, "Honey, we can't go visit Daddy anymore. Daddy died today."

Just like that, he was gone. I remember running outside and tearing up the card, tears pouring down my cheeks and the cool autumn air stinging my face. There are days when I still return to October 22.

I got close to my grandfather after that. But he only lived eight years after my dad. I gravitated to my Uncle Harry because I craved that male bond. He was living with me. I had noticed his breath seemed deeper that morning when I went to wake him up. He didn't want to talk; he didn't want to talk to me, and when I asked him what he wanted for breakfast, he just shook his head and closed his eyes. I sat on the edge of his bed, and I felt so uneasy. After about an hour, I had to get up to go to the bathroom. As I was leaving the room, I heard him mutter, "I love you."

He was not the kind of man that expressed his emotions He didn't have kids of his own, and I was in many respects a daughter to him. I knew this because there are some things we can only see with our heart. Even so, that meant something to me.

"I love you too, Uncle Harry. I will be right back."

His cat, Freddy, was up by his head. I looked back; his eyes were closed, but I could still hear his breath; it was heavy. When I came back into the room nothing had changed. I went by the side of the bed once again and held his hand. I wanted to comfort him, to hold him, so I put my arms around him, and as I did, I could feel the last bit of breath leave his body, and his hand started to get cold.

He slipped away in my arms. That was the first time. I ran to my husband screaming. I was so shaken up. Four years later, my first husband, who comforted me that day, was gone too. With every loss there is grief, and that grief is always different. Society tries to tell us that we need to take time off to deal with our loss but not too much time. There are even stages of grief: (1) denial, (2) anger, (3) bargaining, (4) depression, (5) acceptance. I know them all and a few that the therapists don't talk to us about. Fortunately, we don't have to experience each stage or those stages in any order.

I guess when my dad died, I mostly experienced anger. But I also experienced denial because I had an entire fantasy that he would come back from the dead and ring my doorbell and tell me he had been abducted and brought to a deserted island somewhere in the Caribbean. It was an innocent eight-year-old girl's fantasy. When my grandfather died, I was angry and depressed. When Uncle Harry died, I was angry and depressed. When I lost my first husband, there was a lot of bargaining. You know, "if only I had ..." That's the stuff that really eats at you. The stuff Ricardo helped me let go of.

The worst part is that grief doesn't have a time frame. When I said it is individual, I mean that! And just when you think the twinge of sorrow is leaving, something can happen to have that anguish wash over you like an unexpected rain. If you are like me, the grief of one lost loved one can comingle with the grief of another beloved. Watching death is without question one of the most traumatic things a human can go through. Watching a loved one die is even worse.

The good news—

> The LORD is nigh unto them that are of a broken heart; and saveth such as be of a contrite spirit.
>
> —Psalm 34:18 (KJV)

Think about the stages of grief that are most widely spoken

of: denial, anger, bargaining, depression, acceptance. Have you experienced any or all? If you have, that is particularly good. If you have not, you may just be getting to that place. Maybe you are in one of the stages right now. Understanding them can be helpful. Even after you are in the acceptance stage, you can still grieve, especially during a special day or anniversaries. Take a moment to think about the stages and the questions that each stage asks. This is important because when you recognize what you have felt or what you are feeling, you can overcome or combat repeating the cycle. I have watched death many times. It is an inevitable part of the life cycle. I want you to know that there is not a right or wrong way to grieve. Decide that you will not allow anyone to tell you how or what you should be feeling. You are grieving correctly, and you did not make any mistakes; you are not doing anything wrong. Grief is individual just like all of God's children are unique. Take a moment to write your answers and evaluate where you are.

_____

Denial. Did I experience this and how? Did I refuse to talk about my loss? Am I communicating better now, or do I still avoid dealing with things I need to?

_____

_____

Anger. Was I or am I still angry? Am I irritable, and do I feel anxious? Do I regret things that I say or do after I do them?

_____

_____

Bargaining. What does this look like to me? Am I asking, "what if" and "if only" all the time? Am I willing to do almost anything to alleviate the pain I feel right now?

_____

_____

_____

Depression. Am I eating? Am I sleeping? Am I crying all the time? Am I able to take pleasure in small things happening around me?

_____

_____

_____

Acceptance. Am I now able to understand the reality of my circumstance? Do I know how to move forward from this place without feeling like I am letting go of my memories or somehow being unfaithful?

_____

_____

22

PROVIDENCE

> When thou passest through the waters, I will be with
> thee; and through the rivers, they shall not overflow
> thee; When thou walkest through the fire, thou shalt not
> be burned; neither shall the flames kindle upon thee.
>
> —Isaiah 43:2 (KJV)

There will always be chapters of our life that are written about the struggles. The times when God tested us. These times, when no matter what we do, it did not seem like we did the right thing, that can have a profound purpose. No matter how hard we pray, there will be adversity in our life. Sometimes that adversity is the loss of a job, a financial misfortune, an illness, and on occasion, it is earth shattering—the loss of a loved one.

It's like a tornado that comes spiraling down on our circumstances and blows all those pages in those neat, tidy little chapters completely out of order. God means for us to not be able to change some things. Sometimes that is losing the person we love the most. The prayers don't get answered because God has something else in store for us. Through conversations with God and meditation, I started to understand this.

Have you ever just stepped out on your faith? Took that leap because it was what you believed God wanted you to do? I did.

Without Ricardo, I felt empty in my home, my studio, and my life. I had gotten my health back through exercise and healthy life choices although I was still battling with sleep. I was teaching again in my studio, but it felt like too much. I wasn't happy, and I was not sure if I could ever be again. I was still in that stage of grief we know as depression. However, I knew I didn't want to stay there; I wanted to reach for just a few more moments of joy. Ricardo liked to say, "Life is for the living." I was still alive without living.

I needed to change that state, so I started to investigate why God could have put me in this place again. God crushed my world for a reason. I felt God pointing me south. We cannot hear God's voice, but he does speak to us, and I knew I had to listen. Closing my studio and putting the for sale sign up on my house was difficult—another storm blowing everything out of order, if you will. I was supposed to live in that house with my husband till we were both ready to retire. I was going to run my studio that entire time as well, then leave it to my daughter. I was meant to spend the rest of my life with Ricardo; instead, I had to be grateful he spent the rest of his life with me. It wasn't the story I would have written but God is the author of all things.

Everyone had been telling me to sell the house; it was too big, too expensive, and not healthy for me to hang on to it. The day the real estate agent put the sign on my front lawn, I broke down into tears. I wanted to keep that house. Ironically, it was like God did too. Because most houses in my neighborhood sold relatively quickly, but I wasn't getting any interest. People were not even looking at mine. Yet I knew God was telling me to move specifically to Richmond, Virginia. As I approached a red light while in conversation with God, I asked, "You are sure I should move to the RVA?" I looked at the royal blue Toyota in front of me with Virginia plates. Yes, he was guiding me where he wanted me to go.

The real estate agents had convinced me my house was never going to sell if I was still living in it. The house, beautiful as it was, had too much clutter, too many cats, and a ferocious poodle that bothered everybody that came into the house for a showing. And to make matters worse, it wasn't decorated like a Cape Cod home. It reflected who we, Ricardo and I, had been as a couple. Where we traveled to, what we did, what we loved, and how we lived.

My studio was closed; I had no more income. The taxes alone were too much, and then adding upkeep, landscaping, utilities, insurance, food, car payments. I couldn't make it. God wanted me to go to Virginia. But how?

After my dad died, my mom took me on a vacation to Florida. We stopped in Richmond and a little amusement park still in existence—Kings Dominion. Most kids would have liked that park and Disney World the best, but the highlight of that trip for me was Dogtown. I had wanted to live in Richmond since that very first trip, and I'm not even sure why. But I was going to be there soon; God spoke to me again as I was cleaning out some papers not really paying attention to what I was tossing in the trash. I stopped and asked God to please tell me what to do. The next paper I picked up was from a performing arts program at one of the universities in Richmond, thanking me for sending my students to their summer program years ago. I was unequivocally certain that God was telling me to make the move. The next day, I signed the lease on a small apartment that I had never even been in until moving day.

We packed everything we could into a big U-Haul truck and what didn't fit went into storage. My brother-in-law, Mark, drove down with us. The apartment was small, uncomfortable, and not what we expected. Lonely, confused, feeling sorry for myself, I was officially a resident of the state of Virginia. I had no job, and I wondered how the heck I could have messed up so badly.

Back on the Cape, the real estate agents told me they just couldn't understand why the house still wasn't moving. Then I got sick again: the sore throat, the stuffy nose, and then the cough. I needed the money from the sale of the house to survive. How could I have misinterpreted God's call to action? Before long, the stress of moving, missing my beautiful home, not being able to find a job, worried about where the money for food was going to come from, not getting an offer on my house ... it all caught up to me. My cold symptoms turned into pneumonia. A case that was far worse than the one I was diagnosed with after he passed. Trapped in that tiny little apartment in the west end of Richmond I would have daily conversations with God. Long intimate conversations where I learned how to truly pray.

I remember asking him if I had made a permanent decision on a temporary circumstance, or was I really meant to be in Virginia?

Tagan was attending her last year of high school after having been home schooled for years. She was amazing, making friends, getting involved in school activities, and taking on a part-time job at the pharmacy across the street. I wanted to do better for her. I wanted to give her more than the horrible little apartment where regardless of the temperature, you had to open the slider before you turned on the stove or the fire alarm would pierce your eardrum. I loved cooking. Let me rephrase that. I loved cooking on my beautiful gas stove, chopping fresh vegetables from my community garden down the street, eating on my granite counter while in the next room I could hear CNN softly in the background. I did not like cooking or anything else in my tiny little apartment, so I found myself maxing my credit cards out on takeout food as I painstakingly searched for a job in a city with help wanted posted everywhere.

I was getting depressed and deeply missing Ricardo—the conversations, the physical relationship, human contact. Tagan had made lots of new friends; I had not. The stages of grief do cycle back around; I found myself sitting at a bar across from a man named Tom. He wasn't handsome, but he wasn't unattractive either. He was chubby, dressed kind of drab, and had a receding hairline, but he had a watch on that was worth more than I could make in a year, and his key chain was the Tesla logo. We hit it off and for a moment I thought that perhaps if he asked me out to dinner, I would take him up on the offer. I was lonely; Ric had been gone for close to three years. I was desperate for companionship. He had a nice personality and had told me all about how he had moved back to Richmond to take care of his dad. I thought—nice guy. He listened when I told him about my late husband. Then while I was still sipping the one glass of merlot I had ordered and moving arugula from one side of my plate to the other, we started talking politics. I can't remember the context, but the comment will stay with me.

"You know how Black people are?"

My jaw tightened as I stood up and slapped down my Amex card on the counter. "Yes, sir, I do. I was married to a black man for ten years."

The bartender looked genuinely ashamed as he came back to tell me my card had been declined. I found a twenty-dollar bill in my wallet, some ones and change in the side pocket of my purse. I placed it on the bar and asked if he could try the card for just the remaining balance. The man that had spat out the racist remark that I took such offense to tried to pay my meal, but I wouldn't let him. Racism is alive and well, but I always knew that. My credit cards were officially charged up, and I was broke. Regardless, I could not tolerate certain things, and judging people by the color of their skin was one of them.

> Fear thou not; for I am with thee: be not dismayed: for I am thy God: I will strengthen thee; yea I will help thee; yea I will uphold thee with the right hand of my righteousness.
>
> —Isaiah 41:10 (KJV)

As I said, there are seasons in our lives that no matter what we do, it seems as though it was wrong, and nothing could make our life right again. God sees us in our brokenness and loves us anyway. You may be broken now, but if you stay true to God, he will put you back together. Sometimes, it just takes a little longer than what we want it to.

On my daughter's third birthday, my husband threw her an incredible birthday celebration. We weren't married at the time, but he always treated her like his daughter. After all, he was the only father she ever knew. He even gave her her first bicycle that day. In addition, she got tons of toys including several Barbie dolls. She had a little friend named Olivia that was always kind of fresh. The type of kid that acted sweet to your face but stuck her tongue out at you as soon as you turned around. Olivia had removed each new doll from the plastic boxes and began disassembling them. When I caught her, she had already removed an arm from the Barbie in the bathing suit and the leg off ballerina Barbie. After the loss of a husband, or any loved one, it is easy for us to feel like a fractured doll that cannot be put back together. I felt like that—disassembled—and then it got worse. I was perhaps being tested, as you are maybe now. I did not give up my trust in divine providence, and I pray everyone feeling what I felt, struggling as I did, remains faithful.

The relationship we have with our spouse helps to define who we are. Our husband or wife can transform us for the better and sometimes for the worse. When they are gone, it's like being on a ship that goes off course. Now is a perfect opportunity to discover who you are. Reset goals, think about your own passions, and chart a new course for your life.

You are now on a journey of self-discovery. Transformation requires trials. You don't have to move across country or change jobs to start:

1. Try a new food
2. Get a new hairstyle
3. Try a new hobby
4. Redecorate
5. Buy a dress in a style you wouldn't normally wear

Think about a few things you want to do to discover who you are and write them down here:

_____

_____

23

CYCLES

> And God shall wipe away all the tears from their eyes:
> and there shall be no more death, neither sorrow, nor
> crying, neither shall there be any more pain: for the
> former things are passed away.
>
> —Revelation 21:4 (KJV)

There are people we love and people we depend on. *After* Ricardo died, my niece became a person that fell into both those categories. We talked every day, and our passion to hear about each other's troubles was just as strong as it was to tell our daily narrative. I felt blessed to have her in my life even though she lived in Alabama. When I told her I was moving, she tried to persuade me to move a little further south to Huntsville. In fact, that summer before relocating she desperately wanted me to visit. I wanted to make it down to Alabama; foolishly, I didn't.

As I study the word of God, it becomes clearer to me that we need to live the life Jesus died to give us every day. We shouldn't wait on when—I shouldn't have—but grief has cycles. As God wants us to be filled with joy, he also wants us to find healing in him alone. I needed to learn to become completely dependent on God and God alone to be in the place to truly see what his plan was for me.

After recovering from the pneumonia but still exhausted, I wasn't really doing much of anything. I talked to Debbie for over two hours one day. She mentioned stomach pain several times in the conversation. I didn't really think anything of it but suggested she have a doctor look at her. The next day, Monday, our conversation was much shorter; she was uncomfortable. I used Ricardo as a reference and told her to go to the doctor. Tuesday, I got a call from her when I was in the shower, but when I tried to call her back, she didn't answer. Wednesday the same thing happened. Thursday my sister-in-law, Brenda, called me asking if Debbie was all right. She mentioned some post on Facebook. I was feeling that tightening in my chest as Debbie's number flashed across the face of my phone. Big exhale—everything was okay.

"Hey, Debbie."

It was Debbie's godsister. "Auntie!"

I was confused, and my voice reflected it. "Where's Debbie?"

She paused in between each one of her words, "She had a really serious stroke."

What! No, this couldn't be happening. Debbie had been admitted for stomach pain, and in the process of them running tests, she had a major stroke. There was some damage and considerable water on her brain. She was med-flighted to Vanderbilt Hospital in Nashville. It was too much—guilt, anger, depression, bargaining. She died eight days later.

I needed to be strong. I needed to feed my body correctly, exercise, and rest up because I had to get to her going home. Some things are harder to heal then others, and an already broken person getting beat up a little more needs every promise and miracle that flows through the blood, and that was me. Another crush was too much I was so desperate to heal, but it seemed like the punches kept coming at me. My back pressed up against the wall, legs extended on my bed, holding my phone scrolling through my list of contacts. I couldn't talk to Ricardo—he was gone—and now I couldn't just call up Debbie—she was gone as well. The blank screen of the iPhone dark and cold in my hand seemed useless.

I rang my mother. "Debbie is gone."

She stayed on the phone—silent, simply listening to my sobs.

God was listening too, and I talked to him that night. I cried. I begged him, apologized to him, and then did it all over again. It felt somehow so personal, and I felt deep down in my soul that he was telling me it would all be right with my soul soon. That night I slept, without waking once. I needed that respite because the ride to Huntsville from Richmond was longer than I had estimated.

> Remember the Sabbath day, to keep it holy. Six days shalt thou labour, and do all thy work, but the seventh day is the Sabbath of the Lord thy God: in it thou shalt not do any work, thou, nor thy son, nor thy daughter, thy manservant, nor thy maidservant, nor thy cattle, nor thy stranger that is within thy gates.
>
> —Exodus 20:8–10 (KJV)

I had never celebrated the Sabbath or really understood what made it different than my Sunday service, but several members of Ricardo's family were Seventh-day Adventists. After he died, my niece Debbie, who was a lifelong Adventist, and I were talking about why I had given up pork along with other foods when my husband was sick. I could no longer bring myself to eating them, not that that is why he got cancer. No, the contaminated water at Camp Lejeune was responsible for all that. But most meat repulsed me. When I learned the Bible was clear on what we should and should not consume, I gave up pork and shellfish. Debbie was telling me how she was getting cold cuts at the counter at Kroger's.

I told her, "Debbie, you know your body is your temple, and you owe it to God to take care of that temple."

She laughed. "Auntie, sometimes you sound like more of an Adventist than I do."

I don't think it matters what church you go to, what denomination you are, or if you go to church at all. What matters is that you know God. The Bible is his word, and God's word does not change. The Bible is our true history and our guide to live a life that brings us closer to the Most High.

The first day I entered the SDA Church, which was by

coincidence, I felt closer to God than I had ever been. And he does make things happen because I was thinking about attending a Saturday worship, read some books by Ellen White that a friend had given to me, and continued to have conversations with my niece. Truth be told, I was intimidated. Then my daughter's friend from our Catholic Church called me up crying. She needed a ride, and would I take her to her new church in the morning—Saturday morning. Attending service at Oakwood University Church in Huntsville was familiar.

The home going of my niece was the following day. The memorial was uplifting, the music, for lack of a better adjective, was awesome. To witness how many people came out to pay respects was a blessing for me. Debbie had so much strength and conviction, and she devoted her life to helping others even when she was the one that needed the help most of the time. Her god sister sang, "May the Works I've Done Speak for Me."

> May the life I live speak for me.
> When I'm resting in my grave,
> There is nothing more to be said.
> May the life, the life I live,
> Let it speak for me.

Floods of images flashed in front of me. All the wonderful things that my beautiful husband had done for others; my sweet Nana, who tirelessly took care of me; my brilliant dad; my first husband, who loved unconditionally. Without question appropriate for that day as well because the young people that Debbie mentored came from many different states to speak of her loving heart. I spoke as well, and what I thought would be such a demanding thing to do was not at all. I talked to God about it beforehand. The pastor was truly inspiring, and when they say God has a way to put you where you need to be when you need to be there was proven to me that damp, rainy Sunday in Huntsville, Alabama, because that pastor talked directly to me.

He had such passion and intensity in his voice as he talked about a glowstick. There is only one way to get a glowstick to shine, and that is to break it. Honestly, I really didn't understand how he was relating it to Debbie's passing because my head and my heart were flooded with so many raw, painful emotions. My life, well, it interconnected perfectly with that though. I was that glowstick, cracked and broken because God wanted me to shine.

Driving somewhere in Tennessee on a sun-filled October afternoon, an 804 number came up on my phone. I thought about declining the call. Luckily, I didn't. It was a woman who was opening a fitness club in Richmond, and she needed help. I have been a lifelong mover. A classically trained dancer, I was in a terrible car accident that ended my short-lived career. In London, I met a brilliant Englishman who taught me how to rehabilitate my body through Pilates. Thirty years and at least ten certifications later, it's what I did. This was exactly what I had been praying for. God is indeed good.

I cannot emphasize enough that when we are grieving, it is so important to take care of our bodies:

1. Eating healthy food
2. Drinking plenty of water
3. Using scripture to meditate
4. Finding tools that keep our mind occupied
5. Practicing mindful breathing
6. Exercising

You may feel as though you don't have the energy to do these things, but you don't have the energy because you are not doing them.

Exercise helps regulate your mood. It is a preventative

method to help us, the grieving, from having our grief turn to depression. When we work out, we release endorphins and neurotransmitters that boost our mood. It's a way to combat the need for medication, which may be necessary for some but not for everyone who has gone through a loss. I was deeply grieving and became depressed, but I fought through without sleeping aids, depressants, or anti-anxiety medication because I wanted to regain strength, control my health, and be present for my daughter.

> Know ye not that your body is the temple of the Holy Ghost which is in you, which ye have of God, and ye are not your own?
>
> For ye are bought with a price: therefore glorify God in your body, and in your spirit, which are God's.
>
> —1 Corinthians 6: 19–20 (KJV)

Yes exercise is important but you shouldn't practice yoga. This is a complicated subject. First, let me tell you that when you are in pain, when you feel crushed, you must be so careful with what you allow to come into your life. Now let me tell you the definition of the word. Yoga literally means union. Yoga itself is not a religion, but it is part of a religious practice, and it does affect the practitioner in a spiritual sense. We have all seen the pictures of a young woman in a tranquil scene next to the calm aqua ocean, elbows and forearms resting on the sand, legs straight up to the heavens, and her strong stomach exposed. It's enticing, and we think; "Wow, if I start my own yoga practice my body will become limber, my posture will look so much better, and before long I can be doing inversions on the beach." It seems harmless.

Yoga is so much more than the headstands, the downward

dog, and the warrior pose. I know because I studied yoga and became a certified yoga teacher along with all the other exercise systems, I have been certified in. During my time learning yoga, what I realized was that this exercise discipline wants the person practicing becoming one with themselves, with nature, and with God. There is nothing wrong with that, and for some it can be beautiful and healing; however, as Christians we know we should be one with God. The Bible teaches us that we as Christians should offer ourselves in worship to God not to ourselves.

I have been passionate about my Christian faith as well as health and wellness most all my life. I have worked in the fitness industry for over thirty years. During times of tremendous grief, I embraced movement even more. Stretching was a release of stress and worry, meditating in prayer comforted me, breathing deeply helped combat anxiety that would start building up inside, performing a series of exercises allowed me to fall asleep a little easier. I did these things to renew my body and my mind, but I did them in a way that brought me closer to God because I had already experienced the danger of yoga previously.

In many respects, exercising, stretching, meditation, breathing sounds like stuff you do in a yoga class. But there is more to a yoga class, and I don't ever want to go back to yoga because there is a fundamental difference between being a follower of Christ and yoga. As Christians, it is harmful to delve into this system. I learned this firsthand after getting involved in yoga. I would attend both class and church regularly. At first, I didn't think there was any harm in it.

After a while, I became aware that I was concentrating inward, more on myself. I prayed less; my conversations with God were few and far between. Yes, my relationship with God changed. Then I even started questioning my faith. As I was going through this, my first husband was diagnosed with terminal cancer. Luckily, I pulled back and began rebuilding a bridge to God. I stopped taking class. I stopped teaching yoga as well. I am not saying that my yoga practice caused my first husband's illness. However, it can seduce Christians as it is promoted as a life-giving practice. We need to remember the devil never shows himself as a horned beast. He appears as an angel of light trying to gain access to our lives and wreak havoc on us. The damage it did was try to pull me from my heavenly Father just as I was getting ready to need him more than ever before.

Let me give you a little history of this system. Yoga can be traced back over five thousand years to a sacred text called the Rig Veda. This is written in Sanskrit, and Hinduism, Buddhism, and Jainism have all stemmed from the Veda's. Yoga is not a religion, but it is clearly part of Hinduism. There are what they call eight limbs to the Veda's.

When you first start your practice, you begin with Yama or self-control. The second limb is Niyama, which is a religious practice. You may be encouraged to chant, and these chants are sometimes in praise of Sikh Guru's or Hindu God's. The third is the pose or the Asana and the fourth is the breath or the Pranayama. Climbing up these limbs, you reach Pratyahara, which is the control of the senses, concentration or Dharana and contemplation, which is known as Dhyana. As you approach the eighth and final limb, it is said you reach complete enlightenment. But as Christians we are only supposed to find truth, light, and peace from God.

Here in America, we have turned yoga into commonplace. When I go out to pick up groceries, I go by three different yoga studios. As Christians, many of us deny what yoga really is. But we need to understand that yoga contradicts the Bible and what we are supposed to be doing as Christians. Through scripture, we understand that God values our bodies. Our bodies are our temples, and we owe it to God to take care of them. We can do this without yoga. Once you are healthier, there are other exercise systems that you can learn such as Pilates, TRX suspension systems, weight training, and cardio/dance fusion that do not have any religious connection. But for now, let's put God first and our own self-care and healing.

> The spirit of God hath made me, and the breath of the Almighty hath given me life.
>
> —Job 33:4 (KJV)

24
GLOWSTICK

> O my soul, thou hast said unto the LORD, Thou art my Lord:
>
> My goodness extendeth not to thee.
>
> —Psalm 16:2 (KJV)

The children of the house of Israel were called out from Egypt to take possession of the land promised to them. As the Bible describes it, a land of "milk and honey." This was only to take eleven days; instead, it turned into a forty-year journey. God sometimes takes us down the long hard road instead of the most direct route. Perhaps to test us, to humble us, or to strengthen us. I'm not sure the reason, but I was positive my beautiful, talented daughter, Tagan, wondered why she had to lose two fathers. If God was testing her, she was clearly showing him that she was strong and mature enough to work through his plan for her life despite the pain. She had gotten the part of Christine in an off-Broadway play of *A Chorus Line*, which was being performed in the renowned theater inside the famous Riverside Church. Located in the Morningside Heights neighborhood of Manhattan and across from Grant's Tomb, the NYC landmark has had such notable speakers as Martin Luther King, Nelson Mandela, Bill Clinton, and Desmond Tutu speak, and now my girl's voice would be heard from the same stage. I was excited for her and to step inside that beautiful building. I knew Ricardo would have loved it as well, and without question he would have known more of the history or the architecture and politics of the building.

Late every Friday, Tagan would board the Greyhound from Richmond and wake up in the Big Apple. Sunday night she would catch the bus back, and I would pick her up and drive her to school. She was dedicated and determined. I promised I would drive her the week I was home from Huntsville; we would stay in New Jersey with her aunt and celebrate her performance and my new job.

That Saturday I celebrated the Sabbath with a service and a big vegan meal. Still in shock that Debbie was gone, my prayer for healing was specifically for her mother and her son. I rested afterward. When the sun had set, and I was finally packed, we hit the road. Northern Virginia can be congested, but I thought that leaving when we did would assure, we would not run into traffic.

I turned out of our apartment parking lot heading toward the highway. We passed the Exxon on the right where I usually gas up, but all the pumps were covered in big yellow plastic bags.

"I wonder why the gas station is closed, honey."

"Do we need gas, Mom?"

"No, we can make it to Alex—"

She screamed, "Oh my God."

I had seen it too; a little dark-colored sedan turned right in front of me. Slamming on the brakes, all I could think of was making sure Tagan was okay. I swerved toward the right. If there was impact, it must not hurt my daughter. I remember saying, "Please, God," and hearing the bang.

I woke up to her cries and screams; there was a smell. I pushed the door open and ran around to the passenger side. The door wouldn't open. I could see liquid pouring out onto the concrete.

I yelled, "Get out of the car."

She kept crying, and she didn't move. I screamed again, "Damn it, crawl out now."

People were standing by the side of the road. My head hurt; my knees were burning, yet I walked over toward the sedan. "Are you okay?"

"You hit me."

I did. But she drove right in front of my car, and as a result, I T-boned her.

The EMTs arrived. A tall, nondescript brown-haired man in a uniform asked, "Who was driving that Dodge?"

"Me."

I looked over as another EMT was cracking a glowstick and placing it on the ground. Traffic was backed up around us, and Tagan was standing, shivering, tears dripping down her cheeks.

We were brought into the ambulance, and they laid me down. I saw Ricardo in his blue hospital gown lying on a stretcher. He looked good, healthy, and he whispered to me, "You're going to be all right."

Tagan told me afterward that I had fallen asleep, and not particularly uncommon for me, I was talking in my sleep. Apparently the two things I kept repeating were: "I love you, Babe," and "glowsticks have to break to shine." She was tough, not a scratch on her, and she made it to NYC by bus. I was brought to the hospital. I had whiplash. Considering the damage, I was incredibly lucky. My red Dodge was not as fortunate; it was totaled.

You will know when it's your time to "glow." You will start to feel that life is making sense again. Perhaps you may decide to go back to school, to get a new job, or change careers, to bring awareness to the cause that took your loved one's life by starting a charitable foundation. You may even decide to move to a different state or country! You will begin to recognize your purpose. In the process, you will develop tools to help navigate through feelings of pain and heartbreak. This will make you stronger and more courageous.

Use these questions as a springboard to help you discover that purpose:

1. Is there a way I can use my pain and grief to connect with others who can benefit from the loss I went through?

     _____

     _____

     _____

2. Would I be able to express myself and my feelings better through writing, music, art, or movement?

_____

_____

_____

3. How is God talking to me?

_____

_____

_____

4. Is there still something I must let go of?

_____

_____

_____

5. Am I at the place where I can recognize when I need to ask for help, and am I now able to offer help to someone else who is in pain from loss?

_____

_____

_____

6. How is God calling me?

_____

_____

_____

7. How can I answer that call?

_____

_____

_____

25

R E B I R T H

By *his grace, I found myself in the middle of Manhattan the* following weekend after spending the whole week in bed recovering. I still had a large lump on the back of my neck and some slight brain fog. I was thoroughly grateful to be there with a ticket in my purse to see my daughter perform later that evening. After my near-death experience and truly understanding how fragile life is, how precious every day and every happening is, I was filled with thanksgiving. I lived in the city off and on for years; in many respects, it felt like home. When Ric and I first started dating, I had a small pied-a-terre behind Lincoln Centre. He never really loved New York, so after we got married, I got rid of the apartment. We came to the city a lot, for theater, for shopping, to visit family, just so I could get my Big Apple fix. Consequently, I could easily navigate the streets even with whiplash, so it was nice to just allow myself to wander without worry of getting lost.

Walking west on Forty-Fifth allowed the wind to dance into my face, so I wrapped my bulky navy wool scarf up to my nose so that only my eyes were exposed. I never really liked the cold, but I was happy to be there, skirting around people taking it all in for the first time once again. And there it was right in plain sight.

Crossroads Church

I had indeed come to the crossroads of my life. God has a way of bringing us to where we are meant to be. The crossroads is a place where we occasionally find ourselves standing; two distinct paths lay before us, so we must make a choice. It reflects a place of danger in folklore because as I remember the mythology of it, it was a place where the witches would gather to work their magic, and so there seemed to be some sort of a Satanic inclination to the word, which I did not like.

Symbolically a place where you would not want to hang out long for fear of what it could present.

Robert Johnson, one of the greatest Delta blues singers of all times, sang and strummed the slide guitar about this place:

> I went to the crossroad, fell down on my knees.
> I went to the crossroad, fell down on my knees.
> Asked the Lord above, "have mercy if you please."

It went something like that, anyway. Ricardo sang it to me many times—where legend has it that he sold his soul to the devil at the intersection of Highway 1 and Highway 8 somewhere in Mississippi. He was only twenty-seven when he died. I was not going to sell my soul, and I knew that staying in this place, stuck between these crossroads, could be paralyzing.

There were two choices; I simply could accept what was happening to me. Defeat and failure, I could wander around with the "poor me" mentality; in other words, be that Barbie doll that my daughter's little friend had disassembled. The widow who lost everything. The broken egg with the yolk oozing on the ceramic floor. Satan would love that. And, yes, it would be easy to settle for what I had, nothing. But that was not the hand of cards God was dealing. It was the deception of the devil. I was not going down that road any longer.

I picked the road where I could claim the life God wanted me to have. This would require me to let go of the sorrow that lived in my heart since I was eight years old. To truly decide it was time to heal. It would also mean taking responsibility for myself. Making sure I put God first from that moment on.

I had walked down Forty-Fifth Street so many times before. My girlfriend lived a block west of where I was standing a few years ago. I never noticed it before—the sign or the church. But right here at the Crossroads Church, I knew what I was going to do. Which path was I going to venture down? I had made my mind up, and I had to hurry because the service would be starting soon. I would not give up. I would instead give my heart to him. I was believing; I was talking to him. I was ready. Romans 10:9 tells us, if you declare with your mouth "Jesus is Lord" and believe in your heart God raised him from the dead, you will be saved.

I knelt right there under the church sign on West Forty-Fifth Street between Ninth and Tenth Avenue on the cold, dirty concrete. People briskly passing by me without even noticing what I was doing or what I was saying.

Lord Jesus,

Come into my life fully. I am still in pain; I am broken, and I need your assistance. I come to you as a sinner grateful, ready to repent because I know you were punished for my sins by dying on the cross for me. I also know you rose from the dead so I could have the hope of living forever with you. Thank you for loving me, and know that I believe in you, and I put my trust in you. I am ready to truly understand your word and ready to claim the life I know I deserve as your child. Help me to live my purpose and do the work I was ordained to do.

In your name, amen.

Brushing myself off, I opened the door; there was a young boy that motioned me up the red carpeted stairs. Sabbath school was still going on. In fact, divine worship was supposed to start at eleven thirty, but it wasn't until 12:10 p.m. when a handsome, dark-skinned pastor in silk robe took the mic. "Welcome to Crossroads Church. I am so glad that you could all come; I am honored to share this day with you. As we worship God's risen

Son, it is my hope that God has touched your life and that you will leave this place today with the peace of God inside. It is my wish on this day in the month of Thanksgiving that a few of you will allow us to know what it is that God has done in your life this week to make you truly thankful." I loved the passion in his voice.

I wasn't even sure that I knew I was raising my hand, but there I was in the sanctuary at Crossroads Church standing up with a mic to my lips and the supporting smile and encouraging nods of Pastor Thomas. It was almost as though at that very moment God said to me this is what you have been supposed to be doing all along. I wasn't even nervous. I just started to speak.

"Happy Sabbath, everyone, and thank you all so much for allowing me to be here with you in celebration of this beautiful day the Most High has given us. I truly have so much to be grateful for this week but mostly just to be here with all of you today." Many of the people had turned around and were looking at me. "My name is Sabrina and, you see, last weekend after I attended church in my home of Richmond, Virginia, I was scheduled to drive my daughter here to New York City. However, only a half mile from my home, a car took a sharp turn right in front of my truck. I was told I was so lucky to have stepped out of that vehicle, as they felt most people would have been killed, judging from the damage done to my vehicle. But I know it was not luck but divine intervention, and you can see why I am so grateful to be here with all of you today."

Encouraging eyes from all corners of the sanctuary seemed to be telling me to continue. God seemed to be telling me too. "It is so important to realize the blessings all around us and give gratitude. I realized a long time ago how fragile life is. You see, two and half years ago my husband passed away from stomach cancer. We had something so special, and just like that everything changed. This lesson has taught me that every day is a gift, and we must use it to live a purposeful life, the life that

God has always wanted us to. I know I stepped out of that truck because God wants me to share my story. I appreciate every one of you allowing me to do that today, to express my thanksgiving and blessings to you all."

The pastor thanked me for sharing my story and throughout the sermon referred to me and my experience. After church, I was invited to a fellowship meal. Everyone was so kind to me and expressed their gratitude for the inspiration I gave them. Honestly, I was just speaking life, my life. But for years, people would tell me I had a way of inspiring them with my words and with my strength. I assumed they were just being nice. After all, who was I?

My purpose was not to be a broken toy; it was to be a light. To help others find their way not just to Christ but to peace after life has left them in despair. I was not a broken doll; I truly was a glow stick. A glow stick must be snapped, broken, to be activated. When you do this, you are kicking off the chemical process that leads this object to produce the illumination. God was igniting the light in me, and I had been fighting it. Not anymore, I had been through enough. It was my time to glow.

> You are the light of the world. A city built on a hill cannot be hid. No one after lighting a lamp puts it under the bushel basket, but on the lampstand, and it gives light to all in the house.
>
> —Matthew 5:14 (KJV)

My prayer for you after reading my story is a simple one. That you understand that you are not alone. There is no recovery from grief; we get stronger, and we learn how to cope. We never forget, however. Our feelings become more emotionally stable. I am prayerful that you are able to smile and laugh when you think about your loved one, perhaps even share memories with others, that you enjoy activities you may have stopped doing and you take up some new ones. Most importantly, it is my desire that you are taking care of yourself, exercising, and eating healthy, and that you are looking forward to a bright future for you to "glow" with the memory of your spouse and a heart full of the desire to help others struggling with grief.

EPILOGUE

Have not I commanded thee? Be strong and of good courage; be not afraid, neither be thou dismayed: for the Lord thy God is with thee whithersoever thou goest.
—Joshua 1:9 (KJV)

When I returned to Richmond, I started working and writing my story. I also started to discover who I was. I am a quite different woman than the widow of my first husband. I am also a vastly different person than I was when I was married to Ricardo. We are constantly evolving. They say our body, mind, and spirit change every seven years. I don't know how true this is, but I do know I have gone through immense change spiritually. God sometimes brings us to one place before taking us to our destination. Kind of like a pit stop along the road of life.

Today I call myself a follower of Christ, a daughter of the Most High, partly because I do not necessarily subscribe to religion but to God's word. I celebrate the Sabbath on Saturday as the Bible tells us to in several books but clearly in Exodus 20:8–11 (KJV). "Remember the sabbath day, to keep it holy. Six days shalt thou labour, and do all thy work: But the seventh day is the sabbath of the Lord thy God: in it thou shalt not do any work, thou, nor thy son, nor thy daughter, thy manservant, nor thy maidservant, nor thy cattle, nor thy stranger that is within thy gates: For in six days the Lord made heaven and earth, the sea and all that in them is, and rested the seventh day: wherefore the Lord blessed the sabbath day, and hallowed it."

I study my Bible with eyes wide open, searching for the truth on every page. This has made me realize much of what I once believed is not actually biblical. I follow the dietary laws of Leviticus and work hard to keep the commandments. God's word is God's word, and it is not meant for interpretation. I share my love for God with all who have open hearts. To some I may seem extreme in my conviction, but I have the strength and the spirit to maintain my belief.

I learned the first time the word *church* is mentioned in the Bible is in Matthew. We have formed a concept of what church is. They have been built on tradition and our society. Church is not a building. As it teaches us in Mathew 18:20 (KJV); when two or three are gathered in the name of God, well, that is church.

> For where two or three are gathered together in my name, there am I in the midst of them.
>
> —Matthew 18:20 (KJV)

I am not writing this to suggest that you follow what I do but only to inspire you to learn your own truth and what resonates with your spirit. After the loss of Ricardo, attending church—the community and fellowship associated with it—was so helpful in allowing me to accept God into my life without hesitation. The services I attended were crucial in aiding me to let go of the pain of losing my husband. Loss is difficult. Not one day goes by that I don't think about my late husband, that I don't miss Ricardo and the relationship we had. It is always with a grateful heart. A heart full because my life is better for having loved him; we had something special, something beautiful, and that bond helped to give me the strength to be the woman I am right now.

That woman is hard working, with a reverent heart; she is strong, self-sufficient, and she has learned how to take care of her daughter, her son out of love and herself. Most importantly, that woman loves God. She is me. That doesn't mean that I am not lonely at times. There are nights in my home in Richmond that I wrap up in the quilt I had made from Ricardo's clothing. I feel his arms around me, and I think about all the people I have loved and lost. I miss them too. My dad: my grandfather that I nicknamed DEDE; my Uncle Harry, the first man to die in my arms; my first husband, Nuno; my sweet nana; my beautiful niece. They all played a huge part in my life. I realize they are all inside my heart; their lives influenced me. It's that understanding that also aided in healing my soul.

I am still learning, growing in my biblical truth; things that once seemed so important to me are not anymore; things that I once loved to do, I am not as passionate about, and others I have renewed zest for. I have so many important people that I am grateful for. These relationships are my Lord and Savior blessing me. I focus on that, not what I lost. My faith and trust in him are unwavering. Daily prayer, Bible study and meditation aid in my development. No, the life I have isn't perfect; it never was.

However, I truly feel like that glowstick on the ground; an exothermic reaction has been ignited in my body. The pain, the loss it represents one of the chemicals needed, perhaps the sensitizer. The diphenyl oxalate is the other chemical, I am not a scientist, but I know that is a solid, so it is the strength I get from my faith. Living here in Virginia, I have found so many ways to shine.

> Who is he that overcometh the world but he that believeth that Jesus is the son of God.
>
> —1 John 5:5 (KJV)

What does that mean for me? I am productive—working, teaching, and coaching in my new city of Richmond. Spreading God's word, volunteering, and finding things that bring me joy. Writing, music, painting, cooking, gardening, my animals, simple pleasures like a movie or dinner. I have made friends, and I am now open to the idea of letting love into my life again. You will find you are changing as well; you will discover what you are grateful for, what you enjoy, and what lifts you up. For me, it's God's word, learning my history and the lessons the Bible teaches to sanctify my character. These are things that cannot be taken away.

> Rejoice, and be exceeding glad: for great is your reward in heaven: for so persecuted they the prophets which were before you.
>
> —Matthew 5:12 (KJV)

After my dad died, I saw this book filed with endless pages completely blank except for the faint pink lines that ran horizontally across the soft, smooth surface. The cover of the book looked like a men's jacket in a navy tweed complete with breast pocket. I wanted it because it reminded me of my father. My mom agreed to buy me this journal under the condition that I would decline going to my classmates' "*Chitty Chitty Bang Bang*" birthday party. I realize now she didn't want me to go because it was a sleepover, and she probably didn't want to be alone. At the time I felt resentful that I was forced to choose. Now I understand what she felt; my mother knew me then just as she knows me now. I opted out of the party to take home what would be my very first journal.

Writing after my dad passed gave me peace, and it continues to do so through my life. For over forty years, I have written something down every day. I won't lie; some days it's just a word or an emotion, as I suggested you do. Some days, I pen pages upon pages, and my handwriting is so illegible I don't even know what I wrote, and other days I can be poetic. Regardless, it relaxes me. Writing to bring others closer to the Most High, who gave me the strength I needed to learn to be alone, and the courage to stand up for justice is something I rejoice in.

Going up against the Veterans Administration seemed impossible at first. When I finally had the tenacity to fight for my husband's disability, I felt good. When the claim was denied again, I wasn't as devasted. I know if my husband had been white, I would have gotten his disability benefits and a much better health insurance than I have now. I have lost so much that one more denial could not get me down, and so as this goes to print, I await the Board of Veterans Affairs decision. I pray to God for help not because of financial gain but because my husband, attorney Ricardo Miquel Barros was a proud member of the United States Marine Corps who served his country out of patriotism rightfully or wrongfully deserved. He was injured doing so.

There is a preciousness to every moment. Only some resonate deeply in our hearts. Understanding that love, health, our daily life, life itself is like the petals on a rose. Beautiful, perfect one day, but the next the petals have all fallen off, and we are left with just the stem. There is a deep reason behind cancer, death, any loss. We need to remember it is all a part of life. I know my sweet husband didn't want to leave me. He talked about his unfinished dreams. But God had other plans.

An orbuculum is a crystal sphere. They are stunningly beautiful and come in assorted sizes and colors. When we visited Sedona two years before my Ricardo took ill, he bought me one with a hint of orange in it as a souvenir. The color is so perfect because when I look at it, I am reminded of the majesty of the Bell Rock we stood under on that trip not knowing where we would be in twelve months or twenty-four months. Crystal balls have been used to defraud people since the Victorian era. There is no way to see into the future. Only God knows what path we are set to travel down and for how long. Only those who follow God are equipped to overcome the obstacles that are put in our way.

But for God, I would not have had the audacity to stand up to what I believe to be injustice. Personally, I feel there is medical racism in this country, and if not for that, Ricardo would have been diagnosed sooner. My story is not over, and neither is Ricardo's. I will continue to speak out on the wrongs in our world just as I will of God's goodness. I don't know where God will take my conviction; I just know I will go where he takes me.

After a grueling eight hours of having to recap the pain of the days leading up to his illness, the misdiagnosis, the terminal diagnosis, I was still not done. My head was pounding. I felt defeated. My attorney looked over at me and said, "Great job." Then she said, "You know, it's wonderful that you are doing this." It wasn't for me; it wasn't even for Ricardo anymore. It was because God told me it was the right thing to do for everyone who lost a loved one because of the carelessness and neglect of a broken system that, like so many, judges us by the way we look. Amid this ascension, I am aware that when we are standing at the bottom of the mountain, God is teaching us something different than when we have climbed to the top. Both lessons are necessary.

I pray for each widow; trust God, open your heart to him even if you are still feeling broken, feeling like an unwanted Barbie doll with missing limbs. He will let you shine in his time. Ask yourself, who am I? If you answered: a mother, a father, a doctor, a teacher, a widow grieving the loss of a spouse, a parent grieving the loss of a child, then you are a broken doll. But if you answered, "a Christian, a true follower of Christ," then you are ready because he has a plan for you, and he will take you to the top of the mountain, and he will let you shine. He will make sure you glow.

Sabrina Vaz

is available for private coaching

of both mind and body.

To book a session, visit her website,

www.beautifullybalancedcoaching.com.

She works with clients throughout
the United States and

is also available for scheduled events.

Watch for her companion book,

Moving through Grief,

an exercise program specifically

designed for women

to help learn how to restore their body

after the loss of a loved one.

CPSIA information can be obtained
at www.ICGtesting.com
Printed in the USA
BVHW082028170123
656442BV00002B/240